Clients or Constituents

*Community Action in
the War on Poverty*

NEIL GILBERT

clients or constituents

Jossey-Bass Inc., Publishers
615 Montgomery Street · San Francisco · 1970

CLIENTS OR CONSTITUENTS
Community Action in the War on Poverty
  by Neil Gilbert

Copyright © 1970 by Jossey-Bass, Inc., Publishers

Copyright under Pan American and
Universal Copyright Conventions

All rights reserved. No part of this book may be
reproduced in any form—except for brief quotation
(not exceeding 1,000 words) in a review or scholarly
book—without written permission from the publishers.
Address all inquiries to:

Jossey-Bass, Inc., Publishers
615 Montgomery Street
San Francisco, California 94111

Library of Congress Catalog Card Number 74-110627

Standard Book Number SBN 87589-050-4

Manufactured in the United States of America
    Composed and printed by York Composition Company, Inc.
    Bound by Chas. H. Bohn & Co., Inc., New York

JACKET DESIGN BY WILLI BAUM, SAN FRANCISCO

FIRST EDITION

Code 7002

THE JOSSEY-BASS BEHAVIORAL SCIENCE SERIES

General Editors

WILLIAM E. HENRY, *University of Chicago*

NEVITT SANFORD, *Wright Institute, Berkeley*

Special Adviser in Social Welfare

MARTIN B. LOEB, *University of Wisconsin*

Preface

Clients or Constituents examines the dynamics involved in the development and implementation of the antipoverty movement. The setting for this study was one of the nation's largest industrial cities—Pittsburgh, Pennsylvania; the time was shortly after the antipoverty movement came into existence. I conducted this study while employed in the Research Division of the Mayor's Committee on Human Resources, Inc., Pittsburgh's Community Action Agency. Pittsburgh was one of the first cities to receive antipoverty funds, and the organization grew rapidly, supported by high enthusiasm among the citizens and professionals who participated in the movement. These circumstances—rapid growth and high enthusiasm—created an aura of success, although doubts persisted about the direction in which the movement was headed and about what was being realized.

One major objective of this movement was the democratization of social welfare through increasing the influence of poor people upon the institutions that serve them. Thus the primary effort was directed at transforming clients into constituents. My purpose in undertaking this study was to describe and explain the social forces and relationships that shaped this effort, and that produced at least the interim results. In this endeavor I was extremely fortunate to have studied an organization that possessed a high capacity for internal criticism and a genuine interest in determining how closely its behavior reflected its ideals.

Numerous friends and colleagues in Pittsburgh's antipoverty program graciously contributed their time and talents to bring this study to fruition. I owe a great debt to Norman Johnson, who, as director of research for the Mayor's Committee on Human Resources, Inc., was singularly responsible for making this study possible. His administrative dexterity and personal generosity created, in the midst of an action agency, a work environment that allowed me all of the minor, and some major, indulgences connected with the research and writing enterprise. Special thanks are also due to Chestina Mallory, Louise Starky, and Neil Bush for providing valuable assistance with the field survey, and Renee Sempr for the skill and care with which she typed many drafts of the manuscript.

William Delany and Meyer Schwartz of the University of Pittsburgh, and Camille Lambert, Jr., director of research for the Health and Welfare Association of Allegheny County, offered constructive suggestions on various aspects of the study. I am especially indebted to my friend and gifted teacher, Joseph Eaton of the University of Pittsburgh, for reviewing drafts of the manuscript at different stages and offering his typically penetrating comments. Throughout the study he was a unique source of stimulating discussion and personal encouragement.

I thank *Social Service Review* and *Social Work* for per-

Preface

mission to reprint portions of Chapters IV and VI, which originally appeared in these journals, in revised form.[1]

Finally, I express my deepest appreciation to a community organizer in the antipoverty program who provided me with incalculable assistance and many fertile ideas that I freely incorporated as my own; she was my most ardent critic, sensitive editor, and thoughtful companion—my wife Barbara, to whom this book is dedicated.

University of California, Berkeley   NEIL GILBERT
January 1970

---

[1] "Neighborhood Coordinator: Advocate or Middleman?" *Social Service Review,* 1969, *43*(2), 136–144. "Maximum Feasible Participation? A Pittsburgh Encounter," *Social Work,* 1969, *14*(3), 84–92.

Contents

xiii

Contents

Clients or Constituents

Community Action in
the War on Poverty

Let us suppose that all people take part in government, and that each one of them has an equal right to take part in it. As no one is different from his fellows, none can exercise a tyrannical power; men will be perfectly free because they are entirely equal; and they will be perfectly equal because they are entirely free. To this ideal state democratic nations tend.

Alexis de Tocqueville

CHAPTER I

Democracy and Poverty

Over a century ago Alexis de Tocqueville warned that casting a vote was all too brief an exercise to sustain popular influence on government. Although emphasizing that a democratic system could only flourish through the daily involvement of citizens in the minor affairs of governing themselves, he was not blind to the antinomy that exists between

1

freedom and equality. Alone, the individual citizen is incapable of defending his freedom; in a society of supposed equals, a single voice is rarely loud enough to influence public policy. Consequently, the seeds of tyranny find fertile soil in the state of equality. De Tocqueville recognized that although participation is an essential element of democracy, its form is also vitally significant. To preserve the democratic system, vigorous participation must be coupled with association.[1]

Since de Tocqueville's time, American society has become more complex and human relationships more fragmented. The ability to control the decisions that daily shape one's life has become increasingly more difficult. Giant bureaucracies impinge upon all classes of people. Anonymity is an almost universally felt part of modern life. Yet individuals joined together in groups can, through a consolidated effort, make their voices heard in the political community. They have a relative sense of power and security and will push to extend their interests. Within limits, these "joiners" are still able to influence the forces that shape their lives. However, there exists in America today at least one mass of individuals who are mute, unorganized, and powerless. They have no voice in the political community, no security in their material existence, and no sense of control over their destiny. For this group, the poverty-stricken under-class of society, the democratic process is not real.

POVERTY AND INSTITUTIONAL PERFORMANCE

Theories concerning the noneconomic causes and consequences of poverty tend to be organized around three distinct perspectives—material inadequacy, individual deficiency, and institutional malfunctioning. From the viewpoint of material inadequacy, the individual's lack of resources is considered not only a characteristic of poverty, but also a factor that contributes to its perpetuation. The idea of individual deficiency is derived, in its most primi-

[1] Alexis de Tocqueville, *Democracy in America,* trans. Henry Reeve (New York: Knopf, 1963), Vol. II. For Georg Simmel's discussion of the contradiction between freedom and equality see Kurt H. Wolff, ed., *The Sociology of Georg Simmel* (New York: Free Press, 1950), pp. 66–67.

tive form, from social Darwinism; here poverty is attributed to inherent personal defects. A more modern and less invidious version of this theme focuses upon the culture of poverty; this idea suggests that the cultural and environmental milieu of poverty incapacitates the poor—not inherent biological factors. The third perspective concentrates upon institutional performance, the assumption being that social welfare institutions operate in such a way as to support and nurture poverty. Each of these perspectives is important in understanding the complexities of poverty. Different individuals may view poverty as a function of varying degrees of cultural, material, biological, and institutional inadequacies. These perspectives, separately or in some theoretical combination, are embedded in action programs that seek and often compete for political, economic, and social support.[2]

In the present study the problem of poverty is approached from the perspective of institutional performance. Specifically, the study is concerned with a social movement aimed at providing the poor with an opportunity to influence the institutions that serve them—to make these institutions more relevant to the needs of the poor. This social movement, in attempting to expand the process of popular influence to include the poor, thus relates not only to reducing poverty but also to the broader issue of facilitating democracy.

In the welfare system the poor are generally referred to as clients. This term has two somewhat distinct meanings. The most common usage relates to an individual who employs the services of a professional; but in its Latin inception the term was used to designate "one of a class of dependents attached to patrician families." Although those working in the area of social welfare undoubtedly prefer to be identified as professionals rather than patricians, the system in which they operate functions to reinforce a sense of de-

[2] For a more thorough analysis of these perspectives see Martin Rein, "Social Science and the Elimination of Poverty," *Journal of the American Institute of Planners,* 1967, *33,* 146–163. An imaginative criticism of the culture-of-poverty perspective is given by Charles A. Valentine, *Culture and Poverty* (Chicago: University of Chicago Press, 1968).

pendency in the poor and to inhibit their potential for wielding influence through collective action. The poor are clients in the original sense of the word.

One reason the poor have little influence upon social welfare institutions is that, unlike in most areas of consumption, here they do not have the alternative of taking their business elsewhere. Welfare institutions rarely experience competition from organizations more sensitive to their customers' needs.[3] Indeed, the very idea of duplication of services is anathema to the welfare system. Moreover, the poor as individuals are ill-equipped to demand alternatives. They lack the knowledge and social finesse to cope effectively with bureaucratic officials and procedures. Added to these factors are the frequently overwhelming life pressures that place them in such a vulnerable bargaining position.

Like most large-scale bureaucracies, social welfare organizations strive to maintain conditions necessary to their internal stability. Any disruptions on the part of their low-income clientele are a threat to this stability. Thus these organizations often use their power and skills to limit the political potential of client groups. Dependency and fragmentation are reinforced through the use of "isolative benefits." This reinforcing is done by defining eligibility for benefits in terms of unacceptable role categories or "nonroles": the clients are *un*wed, *un*educated (school dropouts), *un*socialized (juvenile delinquents), and *un*employed. They are also *un*likely to form groups that label them with the role failure such a categoric status represents. Collective action is stymied.[4]

Other procedures that counter collective action and foster dependency involve the manipulation of information and benefits.

[3] This and other factors concerning institutional malfunction are discussed by Harry C. Bredemeier in "The Socially Handicapped and the Agencies: A Market Analysis," *Mental Health of the Poor,* ed. Frank Riessman, Jerome Cohen, and Arthur Pearl (New York: Free Press, 1964), pp. 88–109.

[4] Richard A. Cloward and Frances F. Piven, "The Professional Bureaucracies Benefit Systems as Influence Systems," *The Role of Government in Promoting Social Change,* ed. Murray Silberman (New York: Columbia University School of Social Work, 1965), pp. 49–59.

Democracy and Poverty

In order to challenge or influence an agency, it is necessary to obtain certain facts concerning policies and programs. The highly complex maze of bureaucratic regulations and practices of social welfare institutions provides an excellent jamming device to control the broadcast of this information. The manipulation of benefits is an even more powerful mechanism of client control. In its most blatant form this manipulation simply involves the withdrawal of essential resources as punishment for dissent. A subtler variation is that of selective appeasement; certain benefits are awarded only to the leaders or the most vocal segment of the client population. This maneuver deflates the protest, and the grievances of the larger group remain unanswered. The inhibiting effects of these imperious operations are reinforced by the seemingly arbitrary procedures the poor must go through in dealing with bureaucratic agencies. As a result, the client is overwhelmed by a sense of powerlessness; frustration and fear eventually give way to apathy and resignation.[5] This sense of powerlessness has demoralizing effects upon both the individual and society. It is one source of alienation: the individual moves through life, no longer experiencing himself as the master of his own destiny. He abdicates his rights and responsibilities as citizen in a democratic society and in the end sinks into a state of social and political inertia. When this occurs, society is afflicted with what Saul Alinsky metaphorically describes as "civicsclerosis."[6] The channels of communication and decision-making become obstructed and are eventually choked off.

What if the channels were opened up and the poor given a chance to participate as an organized force in the political arena? As Gunnar Myrdal points out, the integration of these individuals into the democratic system would allow them a more equitable share in the benefits of society and a greater opportunity for self-

[5] See Cloward and Piven. Also see Gideon Sjoberg, Richard A. Brymer, and Buford Farris, "Bureaucracy and the Lower Class," *Sociology and Social Research*, 1966, *50,* 325–337.

[6] Saul Alinsky, *Citizen Participation and Community Organization in Planning and Urban Renewal* (Chicago: Industrial Areas Foundation, 1962), p. 17 (mimeographed).

realization. At the same time, it would strengthen their ties of loyalty and their sense of responsibility to the commonwealth.[7]

DEMOCRACY FOR THE POOR

Providing the poor with an opportunity for political participation is one of the major goals of the War on Poverty.[8] In the development of this program, community action was a central idea. The task force responsible for the creation of the antipoverty bill viewed community action as a mechanism for involving the poor in the political life of the community. As a member of this task force indicates, the observation that "Community Action Programs are a federal effort to recreate the urban ethnic political machines that federal welfare legislation helped to dismantle would not misrepresent the attitudes of the task force."[9] The philosophy underlying this interpretation was supported by the testimony of the then Attorney General, Robert Kennedy, at the hearings held in 1964 by the House's Subcommittee on the War on Poverty.[10] However, beyond Kennedy's statement, which in itself did not present any clear definition of community action, there was little explication of this idea during the hearings.

What emerged from the hearings was a number of implied interpretations of what constituted community action. These inter-

[7] Gunnar Myrdal, *Challenge to Affluence* (New York: Pantheon Books, 1962), p. 103.

[8] The War on Poverty is being used here as synonymous with the Community Action Program (Title II-A) of the Economic Opportunity Act of 1964. There are a total of eleven specific programs under this Act; some, such as the Neighborhood Youth Corps and VISTA, are closely tied into the Community Action Program; others, such as the Job Corps and Rural Loans Program, function more independently.

[9] Daniel P. Moynihan, "What is 'Community Action'?" *The Public Interest,* Fall 1966, p. 7.

[10] Robert Kennedy noted that the poor were powerless to affect the institutions that serve them. He suggested that the aim of the Community Action Program be to change this pattern of relationship by providing real representation for the poor. See U.S. Congress, House, *Economic Opportunity Act of 1964. Hearing before the Subcommittee on the War on Poverty Program* (Washington, D.C.: U.S. Government Printing Office, 1964), Part I, p. 305.

6

pretations ranged from the task force's accent on political involvement to emphasis upon the coordination of services to obtain maximum efficiency in the allocation of welfare resources, the expansion of services to aid the poor, and the stimulation of conflict to mobilize the poor.[11] Stressing the efficiency principle, Marion Crank, Speaker of the Arkansas House of Representatives, told the Subcommittee: "The important new feature in Title II is that it will encourage a coordinated effort toward solving some of the serious problems in our area."[12] Placing emphasis upon the service principle, Robert C. Weaver noted: "The community action programs would focus upon the needs of low income families and persons. They would provide expanded and improved services and facilities where necessary in such fields as education, job training and counseling, health, and housing and home improvement."[13] The testimony of the then Mayor of New York, Robert F. Wagner, suggested recognition, if not acceptance, of the conflict principle. He stated: "I feel very strongly that the sovereign government of each locality in which a community action program is proposed should have the power of approval over the make-up of the planning group, the structure of the planning group, and over the plan."[14] This turbid sea in which the idea of community action floated throughout the hearings was typified by the comments of Representative Perkins (D-Ken.), who continually referred to Title II as the "community facilities provision."[15]

[11] Moynihan, pp. 3–8.

[12] Statement by the Honorable Marion H. Crank, Speaker of the Arkansas House of Representatives, before the Ad Hoc Subcommittee on the Poverty Program of the House Education and Labor Committee, April 10, 1964, p. 3 (mimeographed).

[13] Statement of Robert C. Weaver before the Ad Hoc Subcommittee on the Poverty Program of the House Education and Labor Committee, April 7, 1964, pp. 3–4 (mimeographed).

[14] Statement of Robert F. Wagner before the Ad Hoc Subcommittee on the Poverty Program of the House Education and Labor Committee, April 16, 1964, p. 12 (mimeographed).

[15] Elinor Graham, "Poverty and the Legislative Process," *Poverty as a Public Issue*, ed. Ben B. Seligman (New York: Free Press, 1965), pp. 251–271.

Clients or Constituents

The confusion over community action suggests that the original intent of the "maximum feasible participation" clause written into the Economic Opportunity Act was somewhat vague. This clause specified that Community Action Programs (CAPs)' were to be "developed, conducted, and administered with the maximum feasible participation of residents of the areas and members of the groups served." Despite this nebulous wording, the administrative interpretation of this clause has been fairly consistent in its emphasis upon involvement of the poor in local decision-making processes.[16] At the outset of the program, in 1964, the Office of Economic Opportunity defined the objective of participation in terms of increasing the capacity of the poor to influence public decisions.[17] Shortly afterwards, the implications, if not the effects, of this policy were starting to penetrate the political atmosphere. At the annual meeting of the U.S. Conference of Mayors, a resoluttion was vigorously debated which would propose an amendment to the Economic Opportunity Act, giving local governments greater control over the Community Action Programs.[18] Although this resolution was not adopted, the debate revealed that many big-city mayors were beginning to have uncomfortable visions of militant poverty groups

[16] In "The Community Action Agency and Resident Participation," A Position Paper of the Board of Directors of the National Association for Community Development (mimeographed), pp. 13–27, a case is made against the lack of consistency and precision in OEO's interpretation of the underlying purpose of citizen participation. The authors point out how the wording of this purpose in the *CAP Guide* differs from that in the *Workbook*. However, within the total context of this program, the idea of "achieving a permanent increase in the capacity of individuals, groups, and committees afflicted by poverty to deal with their own problems" (*Cap Guide*) is certainly consistent with the acquisition of "political effectiveness" (*Workbook*).

[17] The objective of participation is discussed in: Office of Economic Opportunity, *Community Action Program Guide* (Washington, D.C., 1965), p. 16; and Office of Economic Opportunity, *Resident Participation* (Washington, D.C., 1965), p.1 (mimeographed). Also see footnote 9.

[18] Advisory Commission on Intergovernmental Relations, *Intergovernmental Relations in the Poverty Program* (Washington, D.C.: Government Printing Office, 1966), p. 54. William F. Haddad, in "Mr. Shriver and the Savage Politics of Poverty," *Harpers,* December 1965, pp. 43–50, notes the reactions of Philadelphia's Mayor Tate to this policy.

wrestling for political power. Under the circumstances, this point of view was not altogether capricious. As the Community Action Programs started to provide employment, legal, and other types of social services, as well as channels of mobility through subprofessional positions, they threatened to undermine many of the traditional functions of the political machine.[19] On the federal level, pressure was also being brought to bear against the enactment of this policy. In November 1965, the Bureau of the Budget suggested that the poor should serve less as policymakers and more as workers in the Community Action Program. However, the Office of Economic Opportunity remained adamant in its position. Its director asserted that he would continue to press for vigorous compliance with the principle of citizen participation in decision-making processes.[20]

In 1966, the U.S. Conference of Mayors reversed its earlier stance and came out in support of the citizen-participation principle. A report issued by the Conference states: "To be genuinely effective, however, participation must involve more than placing representatives of low-income areas on an advisory or policy-making committee. It requires some actual *sharing* of planning and decision-making power with residents and members of the groups served."[21] However, that year the Republican party launched a truculent assault upon the entire poverty program. The brunt of this attack was aimed at misappropriation of funds, excessive staff salaries, and mismanagement of the Job Corps program. Citizen participation in the Community Action Program also received a

[19] In providing personalized assistance through decentralized neighborhood offices, the CAP offers an alternative structure for fulfilling many of the latent functions of the political machine described by Robert K. Merton in *Social Theory and Social Structure* (New York: Free Press, 1964), pp. 73–82.

[20] *New York Times,* November 6, 1965, p. 1.

[21] U.S. Conference of Mayors, *Economic Opportunity in Cities* (Washington, D.C., 1966), p. 26. A survey by a Washington newspaper suggests that this reversal was due to reassurances from Congress that the mayors need no longer fear that federal money would be used to finance new political organizations dedicated to the overthrow of City Hall. Advisory Commission on Intergovernmental Relations, pp. 50–54.

large share of the fire. Political activity related to such participation was strongly criticized: did it mean that City Hall was controlling the poor or that the poor were attempting to alter "the power structure of the city"? The Republicans continued to press that the poverty program be placed under the Hatch Act, a law restricting political activities of federal employees.[22] This attack was carried to the floors of Congress, where, after a much-heated debate, a bill was passed earmarking poverty funds in such a way as to reduce their utilization for organizing purposes and limiting the annual salary of all local CAP personnel to $15,000 out of federal funds. As many CAP directors were earning more than $15,000 a year, some communities faced the problem of maintaining salary levels. One solution was to obtain the additional funds from local governments. This, in essence, put the CAP directors on the city payroll. Thus the salary requirement had vital implications for the control of Community Action Agencies (CAAs), particularly in large urban areas.

Although 1966 was, overall, a particularly inauspicious year for antipoverty legislation, the amendments to the Economic Opportunity Act did attempt to legitimize, if not strengthen, citizen participation. Sections 202(C)' and (D)' of the amendments prohibited any Community Action Agency from continuing to spend funds beyond March 1, 1967, unless at least one-third of its board members were representatives of the poor. The amendments stipulated that these representatives could not be appointed by public officials, or any other agency or person, but must be democratically selected by the residents of the areas they represent. They also stipulated that a procedure must be established whereby segments of the poverty-stricken population—such as minority groups, the elderly, and the rural poor—that consider themselves to be inadequately represented on a Community Action Agency board may

[22] For example, see *The War on Poverty; Who is Winning?* (March 1966), prepared by the staff of the Senate Republican Policy Committee (mimeographed), and *Improving the War on Poverty*, Republican Research Report No. 1, Series A (June 2, 1966), prepared by the Research Division of the Republican National Committee (mimeographed).

petition for greater representation. This mandate on citizen participation was bolstered by a policy statement from the Office of Economic Opportunity, which specified that the requirements concerning low-income representatives on community action agency boards should also apply equally to all major committees, councils, and boards of the Community Action Agency which, although not policy-making themselves, participate significantly in the formulation and implementation of policy and programs, and in the selection of personnel.[23] In reaffirming this controversial commitment to the principle of citizen participation, the director of the Office of Economic Opportunity stated: "The Office of Economic Opportunity funds, delegates, administers, or coordinates a vast array of programs. Every one of those programs can be perverted into a form of dole—paternalistic, unilateral, and degrading. It has become clearer than ever in the past months that the poverty program must stake its existence on that same ideal upon which our nation gambled from the outset: Democracy."[24]

CITIZEN PARTICIPATION

The "maximum feasible participation" clause of the Economic Opportunity Act of 1964 has become one of the most controversial aspects of the War on Poverty. From different perspectives it is viewed either as a threat to the prevailing political structure of the community or as an opportunity for the development of effective social action programs by and for the poor. The idea of citizen participation in federally supported welfare programs is not, in itself, unique. It was a significant ingredient of the Seven Point Workable Program in the urban renewal legislation of 1954. The federal requirements for citizen participation in these programs involved the appointment, by the mayor or city council, of a citywide citizen advisory committee to work with the planners. In practice, these committees initially contained civic leaders representing

[23] Office of Economic Opportunity, CAP Memorandum No. 57, January 11, 1967.
[24] Office of Economic Opportunity, CAP Memorandum No. 49, September 9, 1966, p. 2.

11

various groups and interests in the community. Representation of the poor, who were usually most directly affected by renewal activities, was neither mandatory nor commonplace. But as renewal programs grew and experience with neighborhood-based opposition increased, local agencies began to give greater consideration to participation at the neighborhood level.

However, in most of the instances in which local residents have been involved in renewal planning, their participation has functioned primarily as an educational medium for exchanging views and information with agencies. Involvement in the actual decision-making process has been, at best, minimal. After presenting one of the most detailed accounts available of citizen participation in an urban renewal program, Peter Rossi and Robert Dentler conclude: "If we take the Hyde Park-Kenwood Community Conference as representing the upper limits of effectiveness attainable by citizen participation (as we suggested earlier), then we must conclude that the maximum role to be played by a citizen participation movement in urban renewal is primarily a passive one."[25]

In part, the difficulty in attaining active participation is caused by the frequent penalties that must be paid in renewal programs.[26] As James Wilson notes, participation in urban renewal programs demands a "public-regarding ethos" that predisposes the participants to view an issue in terms of its effects upon the broad community. This ethos is most likely to be found among the wealthier, more educated segments of the community, those who have a cosmopolitan orientation toward life. These people are also the ones who can best afford a "public-regarding ethos," as they are generally not the ones directly penalized by the effects of renewal activities. Their interests, whether related to urban renewal or other public activities, are usually well protected. It is the poor, the uneducated, the people most likely to have a "private-regarding ethos" who live in the neighborhoods slated for renewal. Within this group,

[25] Peter M. Rossi and Robert A. Dentler, *The Politics of Urban Renewal* (New York: Free Press, 1961), pp. 287–288.
[26] See Herbert J. Gans, "The Failure of Urban Renewal," *Commentary*, 1965, *39*, 29–37.

Democracy and Poverty

urban renewal is viewed more strictly in terms of immediate self-interest rather than community improvement. Will my house be torn down? How much will rehabilitation cost? Will I be able to relocate close to my friends and relatives? These are the vital, often survival-linked, questions through which neighborhood people approach the planning of urban renewal. Faced with this approach, Wilson suggests that "if we decide to try to obtain the consent of those neighborhoods selected for renewal, we had better prepare ourselves for a drastic reevaluation of the potential impact of that program."[27] Similarly, Scott Greer quotes a renewal official who has stated, "By and large, people don't understand what we're after —or even what we're talking about. This is fortunate, for if they did, we'd all have to run for cover."[28]

Although scattered attempts have been made to involve residents as decision-makers in urban renewal programs, the emphasis in most cases still remains upon educational forms of participation.[29] In contrast, the requirements for citizen participation in the War on Poverty stress involvement of the poor in policy- and decision-making positions. This concept of participation emerged largely out of the experience of the Ford Foundation's "Gray Areas" programs and the demonstration projects funded under the Juvenile Delinquency and Youth Offenses Control Act of 1961. It is significant to note that the "maximum feasible participation"

[27] James Q. Wilson, "Planning and Politics: Citizen Participation in Urban Renewal," *Urban Renewal: People, Politics and Planning*, ed. Jewel Bellush and Murray Hausknecht (New York: Anchor Books, 1967), pp. 287–301.
[28] Scott Greer, *Urban Renewal and American Cities* (Indianapolis: Bobbs-Merrill, 1965), p. 37.
[29] Pittsburgh is one example of a city in which attempts have been made to involve citizens as decision-makers in the renewal process. For an analysis of the philosophy underlying the Pittsburgh approach see *Citizen Participation: Relationship to Urban Renewal and Planning*, A Report Prepared by the Social Planning Advisory Committee (Pittsburgh: Department of City Planning, 1964). The report is of particular interest because its senior author, Morton Coleman, was later to become one of the major figures in the development of Pittsburgh's antipoverty program, and much of the thinking that went into the role of citizen participation in the antipoverty program appears to be expressed in this document.

13

phrase was written into the draft of the Economic Opportunity legislation largely upon the insistence of Richard Boone, who has been a member of President Kennedy's Committee on Crime and Juvenile Delinquency. The HARYOU (Harlem Youth Opportunities, Unlimited, Inc.) program is among the best-known projects funded under the Juvenile Delinquency and Youth Offenses Control Act. This program directly addresses the issues of political power and social change. Its approach to the amelioration of poverty is based upon developing the ability of citizens in the community "to plan and implement effective social action programs designed to obtain desired social change."[30] Following the leads provided by programs such as HARYOU and Mobilization for Youth, many of the architects and supporters of the War on Poverty recognized that more than a paternalistic effort by the social work community was needed to remedy the structural arrangements that segregated the poor from the mainstream of society. Thus, the antipoverty program was conceived, in part, to stimulate the organization of the poor for the purpose of promoting social change; it was a program planned by professionals to initiate a social movement.

A PROFESSIONAL SOCIAL MOVEMENT

In many respects the antipoverty program resembles a traditional movement for social reform. For example, it is similar to its most recent predecessor, the civil rights movement, in a number of characteristics. The organizational structure is highly decentralized with geographically dispersed autonomous groups loosely coordinated on a national level; the ideology is based upon democratic

[30] Harlem Youth Opportunities Unlimited, Inc., *Youth in the Ghetto* (New York: HARYOU, Inc., 1964), p. 401 (mimeographed). This approach was also emphasized by the Mobilization for Youth program. The proposal for refunding of this program states: "The observers and the organizers of social action have noted that the underlying economic issues are really political issues. Thus the problems of the poor require political action and political action requires power." Mobilization for Youth, *Action on the Lower East Side* (New York: Mobilization for Youth, 1964), p. 68 (mimeographed).

values and beliefs, particularly the idea of equality; and the purpose is to change, but not destroy, the existing structure of social relationships. Although these parallels exist, certain features mark the War on Poverty as a relatively unique phenomenon: a professional social movement.

Social unrest is often viewed as the first stage in the development of social movements.[31] At this stage, certain special conditions must exist to bridge the gap between individual dissatisfaction and collective action. For a movement to emerge, dissatisfactions must not only be consciously perceived and shared, but individuals must also believe in their ability to remedy the situation, and banding together must be both a possible and potentially effective means of promoting change.[32] The unique feature of the War on Poverty is that it did not follow the developmental path of traditional social reform movements. It was not launched out of the depths of mass discontent but, rather, from the heights of bureaucratic detachment.[33] The very fact that the poor were voiceless and could not bring any pressure to bear in their own behalf was, at least indirectly, one of the reasons for the creation of this program.

With a few exceptions, very little public attention was fo-

[31] See, for instance, Francis E. Merrill and H. Wentworth Eldredge, *Culture and Society* (New York: Prentice-Hall, 1952), p. 353; Carl A. Dawson and Warner E. Gettys, *An Introduction to Sociology* (New York: Ronald Press, 1948), p. 690; Joseph W. Eaton, *Stone Walls Not a Prison Make* (Springfield, Ill.: Thomas, 1962), p. 39. C. Wendell King, in *Social Movements in the United States* (New York: Random House, 1956), p. 40, suggests that unrest is more an essential background for the inception of a movement than an actual stage of development.

[32] William B. Cameron, *Modern Social Movements* (New York: Random House, 1966), p. 10. These conditions are analogous to those described under the concept of "dynamic incongruence" by Richard LaPiere in *Social Change* (New York: McGraw-Hill, 1965).

[33] Arthur M. Schlesinger, Jr., in *A Thousand Days* (Boston: Houghton Mifflin, 1965), p. 1011, notes that President John F. Kennedy was puzzled by this political inertia characteristic of the poor. Commenting on this phenomenon, Gunnar Myrdal in "The War on Poverty," *New Perspectives on Poverty,* ed. Arthur B. Shostak and William Gomberg (Englewood Cliffs, N.J.: Prentice-Hall, 1965), p. 122, calls America's poor "the world's least revolutionary proletariat."

cused on poverty in America after World War II. One prominent exception was the then governor of New York, Averell Harriman, who, in his annual message to the state legislature in 1956, called for an "attack on poverty." This proposal was supported with data similar to those cited by the Johnson administration eight years later. However, Harriman's program evoked little reaction and was abandoned by the succeeding administration.[34]

In the early sixties, the Negro protest movement did generate social unrest; however, this manifestation of discontent was born out of racial prejudice and discrimination. Although the highly publicized March on Washington in the summer of 1963 bordered on a direct protest against poverty, the central focus of this movement remained upon the civil rights of the American Negro. Chronic poverty was a marginal issue, but the emotional impact of the civil rights movement did provide an underlying thrust for a war on poverty. Recasting the racial issue into an economic mold was psychologically more acceptable to white America.[35]

National awareness of the poverty problem was intensified around 1960, when Michael Harrington's vivid description of life in the "Other America" sparked a proliferation of literature on the characteristics, effects, and conditions of poverty in the United States. In 1962, two of the five major books published on poverty were on the American Library Association's list of the best books of that year.[36] Although by then the submerged fifth of the nation was becoming uncomfortably visible through the lens of mass media, the middle-class public continued to view social and economic conditions in the overall context of growing prosperity and expanding opportunity. An articulated public demand for direct action

[34] Daniel P. Moynihan, "Poverty and Progress," *The American Scholar*, 1963–1964, *33*, 596.

[35] For a discussion of this issue see Elinor Graham, "The Politics of Poverty," *Poverty as a Public Issue*, ed. Ben B. Seligman (New York: Free Press, 1965), pp. 243–246.

[36] Frank Riessman and Arlene Hannah, "The Poverty Movement," *Columbia University Forum* (Fall 1963), p. 29.

against poverty did not exist prior to President Johnson's State of the Union Address on January 8, 1964.

Unlike in traditional reform movements, the propelling force for an assault on poverty came essentially from within the governmental structure. Only a handful of liberal intellectuals, most of them officials in the Kennedy-Johnson administration, perceived the structural hardening of a poverty class in America. Interpreting the vast fund of information at their command, these officials concluded, among other things, that the gap in income distribution between the upper and lower segments of the population had remained almost constant since 1945; that social disorganization among poor families was increasing; and that economic opportunities for the poor were decreasing. The case for an assault on poverty was, to a large extent, based upon calculated judgments such as these—made by professionals.[37]

[37] Daniel P. Moynihan, "The Professionalization of Reform," *The Public Interest* (Fall 1965), pp. 6–10. S. Michael Miller and Martin Rein, in "Will the War on Poverty Change America," *Trans-Action* (July/August 1965), p. 18; note that "the war on poverty is a political novelty—it does not emerge from the political pressures of the day." Also, see Nathan E. Cohen, "Should Government Take a Direct Hand in Promoting Social Change," *The Role of Government in Promoting Social Change,* ed. Murray Silberman (New York: Columbia University School of Social Work, 1965), pp. 15–22; and Arthur Schlesinger, Jr., pp. 1009–1012.

CHAPTER II

Anatomy of a Professional Movement

In 1964 the federally subsidized attack on poverty was launched in many urban and rural areas across the United States, and the campaign was to be conducted by public and private nonprofit agencies established for this purpose. Pittsburgh was one of the first cities in which such an antipoverty agency was organized. The purpose of this study is to describe and analyze the development of Pittsburgh's program over a three-year period, particularly its efforts with regard to citizen participation.

From a broad perspective, urban antipoverty units share a number of similarities: they have a Community Action Agency (CAA) that is responsible for the overall coordination of the citywide program; program resources are allocated among the city's low-income neighborhoods; these neighborhoods are represented by residents on the CAA Board of Directors; and the residents of these neighborhoods are organized for participation in the program. However, although these broad parallels exist, the internal structure of urban units varies, as does the emphasis placed upon citizen participation.

Pittsburgh is generally considered to be among one of the more successful urban units in the antipoverty movement.[1] This success is judged not in terms of goal achievement (a topic which has not been studied much), but on the fact that an organization was quickly established—one that was able to rally the support of local leaders, to gain the sanction of neighborhood residents, and, perhaps most important, to implement programs almost as fast as the federal monies became available. Pittsburgh was among the first ten cities in the nation to be funded for a Community Action Program in 1964; a year later it received funds more than four and one-half times the amount of the original Office of Economic Opportunity guideline allocation for the city. During the first three

[1] For example, Harry Toland, in the *Philadelphia Bulletin,* June 28, 1965, notes that Pittsburgh is cited by officials in Washington as having one of the best-run Community Action Programs in the country. Similarly, Pittsburgh is mentioned as having a vigorous Community Action Program and as being among the outstanding examples of antipoverty programs that have gotten off to a smooth start in Alfred Friendly, *The Better War: As Reported by The Washington Post, Associated Press, The Cincinnati Enquirer, and United Press International* (Washington, D.C.: U.S. Government Printing Office, 1966), pp. 49–50, 73–74.

years of operation of the Pittsburgh program, its fiscal integrity was above reproach; the program was cited by Sargent Shriver as a national model; and it was favorably evaluated by the press. These accomplishments stand up well when compared with the records of other major urban antipoverty units.

There are numerous paths along which to approach a descriptive study of phenomena as intricate, and yet as elusive, as social movements. As no one exploration can be expected to map every trail or describe every aspect of this vast terrain, certain limits and directions were placed upon the focus of this study. Specifically, the study analyzes six elements of a professional social movement: organizational structure, strategy for change, professional leadership, solidarity, opposition, and goal achievement.

These categories were chosen for a number of reasons, both theoretical and practical. A theoretical reason is that once the organizational structure emerges, the accomplishment of a movement's initial objectives is closely related to the degree of solidarity and the intensity of opposition. No formula exists by which to calculate the precise relationship between solidarity and opposition. However, certain judgments can be made concerning the extent to which these variables may affect goal achievement. For example, the coupling of intense opposition with a low degree of solidarity suggests that the movement will be forced to alter significantly its initial objectives or suffer annihilation. Organizational structure is an important consideration because it provides a framework that may facilitate or impede the development of solidarity and the implementation of strategy. The significance of strategy for promoting change is twofold: it provides a criterion for judging the coherence of the organization, and it accounts, in part, for the emergence of opposition. For example, a conflict-oriented strategy is more likely to invoke serious opposition than one based upon the principle of accommodation, and a strategy of swift and total action is not coherent with a loose and decentralized organization. Finally, the very nature of a professional movement suggests that a clear understanding of this phenomenon will not emerge without some knowledge of the professional leadership.

Anatomy of a Professional Movement

These five elements—structure, strategy, solidarity, leadership, and opposition—are closely interrelated. The leadership molds the structure, and the structure may thwart the leaders; the structure may facilitate or impede the development of solidarity and the implementation of strategy; strategy may operate to increase or reduce opposition; a moderate degree of opposition may function to increase solidarity, whereas more intense opposition may have the opposite effects. The dynamic interaction of these five elements is in the main responsible for producing the sixth element, that of goal achievement. Thus, from a theoretical perspective, the rationale for organizing this study around structure, solidarity, leadership, strategy, opposition, and goal achievement is that these elements are closely linked and crucial to understanding the dynamics of a professional social movement.

The practical, and perhaps more compelling, reasons for choosing these categories have to do with the investigator's personal experience during almost four years of community-organization and research work at both the "grass roots" and "downtown" levels in Pittsburgh before and during the development of the War on Poverty program. Implicit in the categories are many questions that were raised only to remain shadowed in half-answers during this period. Are most of the participants poor? Do they identify with the poor? Do they possess a common ideology? Do they understand the strategy for change? How do they perceive the role of professionals? To whom are the professionals responsible? Is the strategy for change effectively utilized by citizens? How does the structure of the antipoverty program affect strategy and objectives? Where are the potential sources of opposition? These are a sample of the questions that will be addressed in the course of this study.

ORGANIZATIONAL STRUCTURE

From the beginning of the War on Poverty, the local community, generally defined in terms of a major political jurisdiction such as county, city, or town, was viewed as the key operating unit. The idea of maximum local initiative in the development and implementation of the antipoverty effort was explicitly stressed during

21

the legislative hearings. As explained in the House Committee report:

> This is based on the belief that local citizens know and understand their communities best and that they will be the ones to seize the initiative and provide sustained vigorous leadership. It is based, too, on the conviction that communities will commit their ideas and resources and assume responsibility for developing and carrying out local programs. Thus, the role of the federal government will be to give counsel and help, when requested, and to make available substantial assistance in meeting the costs of the programs.[2]

Within an urban community the organizational structure of the operating unit may be viewed on two levels: downtown and neighborhood.

The Downtown Agency. The Economic Opportunity Act defines a Community Action Program, in part, as a program "which is conducted, administered or coordinated by a public or private nonprofit agency (other than a political party), or a combination thereof." This Community Action Agency (CAA) is the command headquarters of the urban unit.

During the legislative hearings in 1964, Congress rejected the idea that these CAAs must be "broadly representative" or that they must involve "maximum feasible participation of public agencies and private organizations primarily concerned with the community's problems." The intent here, it appears, was to allow other than broadly based agencies the opportunity to receive funds.[3] However, the Office of Economic Opportunity did not encourage this practice. In the instructions for developing a community action program, it is indicated that "the most effective and desirable community action program is one which is broadly based, organized on a community-wide basis, and involves the coordination of a variety of antipoverty efforts." These instructions also set forth the organizational model for CAAs. The model prescribes a fairly large gov-

[2] National Association for Community Development, *The Community Action Agency and Resident Participation,* A Position Paper of the Board of Directors of the National Association for Community Development, p. 2 (mimeographed).

[3] National Association for Community Development, p. 3.

erning board made up of three categories of representatives: *Private and public agencies*—at least one representative of the elected officials of the community, the board of education, the public welfare agency, and major private social service agencies; also to be considered are the public health agency, the urban renewal agency, the public housing agency, the local office of the State Employment Service, and other agencies working with the poor. *Community leaders*—local leaders of labor, business, minority groups, and religious groups. *Residents of the areas and members of the groups to be served*—at least one representative from each of the community action program target neighborhoods. Whenever feasible, these members should be selected through traditional democratic processes.[4]

In 1966 this prescription was slightly altered. Regarding the public and private agencies, the minimum requirements were reduced to representatives of the chief elected officials of the community (such as the mayor or city councilmen, city or county commissioners)' and elected school officials. According to this requirement, representation of public welfare agencies and major private social service agencies along with public housing agencies, urban renewal agencies, public health agencies, and so on should be considered, but is not mandatory. Concerning citizen participation, the original prescription speaks of "representatives of the residents of the areas and groups to be served." As the areas to be served usually contain residents of various income levels, this requirement allowed for broad-based economic representation. The new formula stipulates that the citizen delegates be "representatives of the *poor persons* [italics added] who are residents of the areas and members of the groups [served]." It also specifies that they must comprise at least one-third of the CAA governing body.[5] While these representatives need not themselves be poor, "they must be selected in a manner that insures that they truly represent the poor."

[4] Office of Economic Opportunity, *Community Action Program Guide* (Washington, D.C.: Office of Economic Opportunity, 1965), Vol. I, pp. 16–18.
[5] Office of Economic Opportunity, *Community Action Memorandum No. 57,* January 11, 1967, p. 3.

Clients or Constituents

This overall organizational model has been criticized from a number of perspectives. One criticism is that the model was dictated by the Office of Economic Opportunity rather than allowed to emerge through the experience and initiative of the local communities. Another relates to the fact that the model requires a confederation of interests to be represented on the CAA governing board. In this type of structure there is a distinct tendency for conflicting interests to balance each other out. The results, as experience with health and welfare councils testifies, are generally not conducive to stimulating community change. The National Association for Community Development suggests that the OEO prescription may be suitable for dividing up the new federal funds, but "it will mean playing down the role of catalyst and change agent."[6]

Neighborhood Councils. Whereas only a limited number of residents can participate on the CAA boards, the neighborhood level offers an opportunity for mass participation. The neighborhood citizens' councils are the field regiments for the War on Poverty. It is these groups that can form the active constituency of the antipoverty movement.

The structure and functions of the neighborhood citizens' councils vary from city to city. One observer of resident participation in ten cities across the nation reports that "in half the cities— Durham, Washington, Pittsburgh, San Francisco, Oakland—the residents' organizations being formed in old neighborhoods through the poverty program were enlightened independent organizations with some strength." But in other cities, such as Chicago, Cleveland, and Rochester, these organizations were feeble puppets of the administration; they had "no independence, no power, and no push." In Chicago the neighborhood-center directors, who were employed by the city government, appointed 80 per cent of the members of the residents' councils. Mayor Locher of Cleveland discouraged participation by giving the neighborhood councils no powers and ignoring them during the riot period.[7]

[6] National Association for Community Development, p. 8.
[7] James V. Cunningham, *Toward a Loyal Urban Opposition,* A

Anatomy of a Professional Movement

Where the local CAA delegates some policy-making functions to these groups, the Office of Economic Opportunity requires that at least one-third of these councils' governing bodies consist of democratically elected representatives of the poor. Other requirements concerning residents' organizations are, in some instances, set locally. For example, to be recognized in Pittsburgh as an official War on Poverty unit for its neighborhood, a citizens' organization must meet the following criteria: (a) Be representative in terms of residence, business and commercial institutions, race, income (especially low income), sex, and other neighborhood groupings. Be committed to continually increasing its representative character. (b) Be familiar with the city's community action program and committed to its basic goals. (c) Be an advocate for the poor in the organization's neighborhood and also committed to developing a good system of communication with the poor. (d) Be composed of officers and members prepared to commit a great amount of time and effort. (e) Clearly understand the powers and responsibilities it is assuming. (f) Begin building an organization that through its membership or through attendance at meetings directly involves a sizeable proportion of the residents of the neighborhood. (g) Further demonstrate its ability to reach and involve people in the neighborhood through raising of funds each year to assist in carrying out its functions. (This provision was not strictly enforced.)

Pittsburgh has appeared to make a concentrated effort to encourage participation at the neighborhood level. The citizens' councils are, theoretically, responsible for planning, implementation, and evaluation of local services.

ROLE OF PROFESSIONALS

The paid organizers are the field lieutenants of the antipoverty movement.[8] Although they have been recruited from all

---

summary report to the Ford Foundation on resident participation in urban antipoverty programs, October, 1966, pp. 9–10 (mimeographed).

[8] Although the discussion here of professional role focuses on these neighborhood-based field lieutenants, the issues involved are similar, macro-

walks of life, the majority come from the more militant social work community, the civil rights movement, and the Peace Corps. In most cities these organizers are either on the staff of the Community Acttion Agency or are contracted out by the Community Action Agency to local organizations; in a few instances these contracts have been given directly to citizens' groups that have incorporated into nonprofit organizations.

Faced with the dual goals of expanding service and stimulating institutional change, the organizers are often caught between the Scylla of attempting to coordinate the delivery of service and the Charybdis of trying to alter the welfare structure. Theoretically, the functions of coordination and alteration are not necessarily opposed; but in practice, the potential for conflict is very strong. The function of coordination is essentially that of an expediter attempting to increase both the demand and supply sides of the service equation. Here the organizer works with and supports both citizens and agencies. The function of alteration involves working with and supporting only the citizens, the emphasis being upon changing the welfare structure.

Middlemen or advocates? This question involves practical as well as philosophical issues. The middleman provides the "cement that binds distributors and consumers"; his mode of operation is based upon the cooperative approach to social planning.[9] From a practical stance, this position is politically viable. Federal funds are not being used to attack or disrupt the activities of local agencies. The middleman is neutral.[10]

Although neutrality is politically innocuous, it is a difficult position to maintain in pluralistic society. As with many groups of

scopically, for the "generals" downtown. Throughout the study, the downtown professionals' roles are implicitly assessed in similar terms.

[9] Martin Rein and Frank Riessman, "A Strategy for Anti-Poverty Community Action Programs," *Social Work,* 1966, *11*(2), 6.

[10] For a further analysis of the issues concerning the role of the organizer see Frank Riessman, "Antipoverty Programs and the Role of the Poor," and the discussion by Paul Jacobs, Jean C. Cahn, and Edgar S. Cahn, which follows the Riessman article, in *Poverty in America,* ed. Margaret S. Gordon (San Francisco: Chandler, 1965), pp. 403–428.

consumers and suppliers, the interests of the poor frequently do not coincide with those of the welfare system. Welfare institutions strive to maintain control over the allocation of scarce resources. When the demand of the poor for those resources outstrips the supply normally allocated to them, neutrality is often shattered. If the middleman attempts to avoid overloading the system by placing a lid on demand, he has "sold out to the establishment"; the trust and confidence of the consumer is lost. If he chooses to support consumer demands, he is labeled an "agitator" by the welfare agencies. In either case, once a position is taken, it is difficult to regain the balance of confidence necessary to continue in the role of an expediter. The problem of maintaining a neutral stance is compounded by the structure of most antipoverty units. The organizer is on the payroll of either a Community Action Agency, which is often politically controlled, or a local welfare organization; he is, to begin with, an agent of the "establishment." From this position, claims to neutrality are, with good cause, suspect.

Some modifications in the welfare system may come about in the process of coordinating the delivery of services. Historically, however, the vast majority of significant changes in our society have occurred as a result of political or economic pressure, the influence wielded by groups acting in their own self-interest. Major institutional change is unlikely to take place without resistance. The very notion of change implies movement; movement creates friction; friction generates heat. In this vein, Edgar Cahn suggests that the role of the organizer ought to involve stimulating "the voices of grievance and of protest in such a way that 'heat' is put on local agencies, so that they would turn to their local sources of support and say that in a democracy it is your job to respond."[11] The problem with this position, as evidenced by the independently funded and militant Syracuse Community Development Association, is that the response is often dictated by political expediency—organizing funds are simply cut off.[12]

[11] Margaret S. Gordon, ed., *Poverty in America* (San Francisco: Chandler, 1965), p. 428.
[12] For two views on the Syracuse incident see Nicholas Rezak, "The

Clients or Constituents

In terms of practical consequences, it is difficult to determine which role is more feasible to maintain. Both the advocate and the middleman may be able to walk the tightrope between "political agitator" and "establishment fink." With resourcefulness, tact, and skillful negotiation, the middleman may be able to maintain the confidence of the consumer without alienating the supplier of welfare services. Through coordination he may be able to develop a more rational and effective service system; and in this process the system may be voluntarily altered to some degree. Similarly, the advocate, with the support of an independent and courageous Community Action Agency, may be able to increase demand, alter the allocation of welfare resources, and significantly change the structure of the system. In either position the organizer runs the risk of being "cut off," the middleman through the loss of citizen support and the advocate through the loss of institutional sanction. In attempting to maintain a balanced position much depends upon the local political structure, its tolerance of dissent, and its ability to withstand stress.

The philosophic issue concerning the role of the professional relates not to the feasibility of maintaining a specific position, but to the desirability of that position in light of the principles underlying the antipoverty movement. If the essential objective of citizen participation is to facilitate the administration of services to the poor, then bridging the gap between consumers and suppliers is obviously a desirable end. But if the objective is to stimulate participatory democracy, to strengthen the influence of the poor over decisions which affect their lives, then the very nature of a pluralistic society dictates that the professional represent and support the interests of this group.

DEMOCRATIZATION OF SOCIAL WELFARE

It would not be difficult to muster a general consensus among those who framed and supported the Economic Opportunity

Use and Effectiveness of Conflict as an Instrument of Social Change," *Community*, 1966, *42*(1), 10–13 and Jules Witcover and Erwin Knoll, "Politics and the Poor: Shriver's Second Thoughts," *The Reporter*, December 30, 1965, pp. 23–25.

Anatomy of a Professional Movement

Act of 1964 that this program was designed for the ultimate purpose of eradicating poverty. But the nobility of "ultimate purpose" is frequently used to obscure a movement's more specific and sometimes less than noble objectives. Take, for example, the eugenics movement; is there any purpose more estimable than that of perfecting humanity?

As reflected in the Congressional discussions on community action, the specific objectives underlying the War on Poverty may be divided into two categories. Those who interpreted the idea of community action in terms of the expansion and more efficient allocation of services implicitly supported a category of objectives that center upon the principle of *individual change*. The notion here is that the poor lack certain characteristics requisite to achieving success in the competitive arena of middle-class America. The main objective is to rectify these deficiencies through the provision of health, legal, occupational, educational, and social services. Other objectives implicit in this category involve the promotion of social control and uniform standards of behavior.

The second category of objectives is suggested by those who interpreted community action as signifying an attempt to increase the political power of the poor. In this category the central principle is the *democratization of social welfare*. Poverty is understood not just as a lack of material goods, but also as a sense of impotency and a lack of dignity and self-respect. This principle includes the assurance of civic as well as economic self-sufficiency. Here the main objective is to involve the poor not only as clients of welfare services, but also as participants in the planning and implementation of these services. This involvement implies a change in the decision-making structure of the institutions that serve the poor, one that would allow them access to this structure and permit influence upon the decisions made therein, thus providing leverage to obtain a more equitable redistribution of goods and services. Another objective implicit in this category is the promotion of individual self-realization. An article of faith basic to democratic theory is that people "must be allowed a share in political control because to

29

command obedience without free participation in control is to deny the right of all to self-development through responsibility for their own acts—is to reduce men to the degrading irresponsibility of slaves or mules."[13]

Although the democratization of social welfare and individual change are not antithetical objectives, at certain points there is a strong potential for conflict between them. As Martin Rein and S. M. Miller indicate:

> Participatory democracy conflicts with the goal of promoting harmony, at least in the short run. If welfare programs are designed chiefly to promote social control and to reduce conflict and tension in the community, then the involvement of the poor in shaping policy, which may have the effect of involving them in boycott, pickets, strikes, and other forms of protest which dramatize their grievances, produces tension and conflict.[14]

The objective of individual change reflects the traditional approach of the social welfare establishment toward poverty in America. It offers little more than a federal expansion of the community welfare council concept; that is, increased efficiency, improved planning, and expansion of services. In contrast, the democratization of social welfare implies significant changes in the structure of the welfare system and the allocation of its resources. Consequently, this objective presents a more relevant standard for judging the achievements of the War on Poverty as a professional movement for social reform.

The interrelationship between goal achievement and the other five elements of a professional social movement is implicitly discussed throughout this study. In Chapter IX these relationships are summarized, and the element of goal achievement is examined from a dynamic perspective.

[13] John D. Lewin, "The Elements of Democracy," *Analyzing Social Problems,* ed. John E. Nordskog, Edward C. McDonagh, and Melvin J. Vincent (New York: Dryden Press, 1950), p. 588.

[14] Martin Rein and S. M. Miller, "Poverty Policy and Purpose: The Axes of Choice," *Poverty and Human Resources Abstracts,* 1966 *1*(2), 17.

Anatomy of a Professional Movement

The democratization of social welfare is, in essence, predicated upon the idea of citizen participation. This idea encompasses a broad range of activities that take place in a number of organizational settings. A few examples are: church organizations distributing food baskets at Christmas; volunteers making door-to-door collections for the community chest; PTA members planning a charity sale; civil rights advocates marching on Washington; or neighborhood groups petitioning city council for better police protection. The three criteria that distinguish these activities as "citizen participation" are: *Organized effort*—a spontaneous mass action is not considered a form of citizen participation. *Utilization of volunteers*—the activities involved cannot constitute a source of livelihood for the citizen participants, as in the case of professional pickets.[15] *In the public interest*—the public interest may be broadly defined to include a nation, a state, a community, a social class, an ethnic group, and the like, but it does not involve private monetary profit.

Although these criteria, in very general terms, define the parameters of the concept, a further refinement is necessary: the broad range of activities falling under the rubric of citizen participation may be divided into two categories:[16] *Social service*—providing various types of voluntary service in the public interest, such as supervising playgrounds, making charity collections, and

---

[15] Some claim that nonprofessional employment in the antipoverty program is an example of citizen participation. Although it has been one of the program's more creative aspects, the work done by salaried nonprofessionals is not, for the purposes of this study, considered to be citizen participation. These staff are drawn from the low-income segments of the antipoverty neighborhoods, but their participation is generally dictated by agency policies.

[16] This dichotomy is implicitly suggested by Michael Harrington in "The Politics of Poverty," *The Radical Papers*, ed. Irving Howe (New York: Anchor Books, 1966), pp. 143–144. He distinguishes between community organization for "self-help, neighborhood uplift" and organization for political action. The former involves organizing people to help clean up their block; the latter suggests pressuring City Hall for improved public services.

cleaning up vacant lots; and *Social action*—attempting to influence public decisions.

It is in the latter sense of social action that the concept of citizen participation relates to the democratization of social welfare. Within a social action context, citizen participation may serve a number of functions. For analytic purposes these functions may be broken down into four categories moving from the most passive to the most active functions of participation.[17] The first two functions are "passive," inasmuch as the influence on public decision-making is vague, indirect, and, at best, slight. They generate no sense of power and have little real effect on the democratization of social welfare.[18] These functions are: *Stimulation of citizen awareness of a problem*—basically, this involves a one-way educational process whereby, through various methods such as self-survey, mass media, and "explanatory" meetings citizens gain information about a problem that requires public action. Here citizens are either talking to themselves or being talked to. When the citizens start talking to the public decision-makers, the function of participation moves into the next category. *Creation of a climate of opinion which* indirectly *shapes public decisions*—this is primarily a two-way educational process whereby citizen awareness is not only stimulated, but, through methods such as public hearings and "confrontation" meetings, the citizens are also allowed to exchange opinions and information with public officials.

The two "active" functions of citizen participation involve

[17] In reality, the dividing lines between these functions are often blurred, as the forms of participation may alter over time. Peter M. Rossi and Robert A. Dentler, in *The Politics of Urban Renewal* (New York: Free Press, 1961), pp. 284–287, discuss these functions in terms of different phases of participation in the planning process.

[18] Frances F. Piven suggests that a significant difference between citizen participation in urban renewal and participation in the War on Poverty is that renewal programs emphasize "educational forms of participation," whereas in the poverty program participation is geared to enhance "the effective influence of low-income people on the policies and practices of institutions that serve the low-income community." See "Participation of Residents in Neighborhood Community Action Programs," *Social Work*, 1966, *11*, 74–75.

some measure of influence on public decision-making.[19] They are: *Creation of a broad citizen base for the support or rejection of a public decision*—here participation functions primarily as a mechanism for legitimizing public decisions. The process might be termed "democracy by veto," since real influence is only exerted when the citizens reject a public plan. In practice, this is often not an all-or-nothing situation. Plans that are rejected may be modified and again brought before the citizens. When this occurs, the function of participation moves into the next category. *Actual shaping of public decisions*—here the citizens operate either within the system in a decision-making position, such as sitting upon planning boards; or outside the system, negotiating with its representatives about various decisions that affect their lives. This is the most active function of citizen participation since the influence upon decision-making is direct and forceful.

Although no absolute criteria exist by which to measure the achievement of democratization, this active-passive continuum of participation by the poor in the process of public decision-making offers one standard for judging the degree to which this objective is realized. Commenting on this issue, Edgar and Jean Cahn suggest that if the War on Poverty is to accomplish a meaningful victory, "the ultimate power to govern must not only reside with the governed, but . . . such power must be susceptible to continuous and effective, rather than nominal and sporadic, exercise. It must include both the power to give and withhold assent. The ultimate test, then, of whether the War on Poverty has incorporated the 'civilian perspective' is whether or not the citizenry have been given the effective power to criticize, to dissent, and where need be, to compel responsiveness."[20]

---

[19] In relation to the analytic framework presented by Edgar and Jean Cahn, the passive functions of participation correspond to the view of the War on Poverty as a "military service operation." The active functions involve the incorporation of a "civilian perspective" into this program. See Edgar S. Cahn and Jean C. Cahn, "The War on Poverty: A Civilian Perspective," *The Yale Law Journal*, 1964, 73(8), 1317–1352.

[20] Cahn and Cahn, p. 1329.

Clients or Constituents

Solidarity is one of the key variables that distinguish the professional social movement from the traditional type of reform movement. The idea of solidarity brings to mind a number of meanings associated with the concept of cohesiveness, such as a sense of group loyalty and a feeling of "we-ness." However, the concept of cohesiveness, although open to various interpretations, is generally limited by sociologists to refer to the phenomenon of attraction to the group.[21] Solidarity, as used here, refers to the phenomenon of voluntary cooperation of group members. Both of these concepts are interrelated, as forces that influence cohesion often have a similar impact upon solidarity—that which attracts members to participate often predisposes them to cooperate.

The professional social movement is launched through a formal organization structured (by the professionals) to foster the development of solidarity. The traditional movement, through a more gradual development, is inherently predisposed to achieving solidarity because of the consciously perceived and shared discontent of its members. Also, it is often faced with an identifiable source of conflict that functions to increase this solidarity.

Some of the key factors that influence the degree of solidarity within a social movement are: incentives related to psychological or material satisfaction of members, external conflict, and membership characteristics. While incentives and external conflict are factors that may operate to support the structure of solidarity, it is the membership characteristics that provide the essential foundation upon which this structure is built.[22] These characteristics are: congruent membership, group identification, and common ideology.

Congruent Membership. This term is not meant to suggest

[21] For example, see Dorwin Cartwright and Alvin Zander, *Group Dynamics* (Evanston, Ill.: Row, Peterson, 1953), pp. 73–90.

[22] As Lewis Coser points out, if a certain degree of solidarity does not exist prior to the outbreak of external conflict, it is likely that this conflict will result in the disintegration of the group. See Lewis Coser, *The Functions of Social Conflict* (New York: Free Press, 1964), pp. 87–95.

that members of a movement must in every case belong to a homogeneous group. Rather, it implies a correspondence between the membership and the achievement of the movement's objectives. As Ralph Turner and Lewis Killian indicate, when the objectives appeal to the self-interest of a particular segment of society, this appeal insures not only "a vigorous rather than lip-service support from a group of people, but it also gives the movement access to the preestablished organization and communication networks of a group with some preexisting homogeneity."[23] Depending upon the scope of a movement's objectives, congruency might involve a high or low degree of homogeneity. As the civil rights movement demonstrates, the notion of congruency may change as the objectives shift; here, for example, white leadership is becoming incongruent as the emphasis upon "black power" emerges.[24] Because the poor are a diverse group, achievement of congruent membership is particularly relevant to the War on Poverty. Solidarity may be weakened if a disproportionate number of citizen participants are not the poor themselves, or if they are drawn from only limited segments of the poor population, such as the Negro, the working class, or the elderly. In the first case, it is obvious that the middle-class planning of social welfare programs does little in the way of fostering democracy for the poor. In the second case, the membership does not correspond to the achievement of the movement's objectives in that it arbitrarily limits the population base from which support and cooperation may be drawn.

As a result of the shared discontent out of which traditional movements emerge, they have less difficulty than professional movements in attracting congruent membership. In compensation for this inherent shortcoming, the planners of the War on Poverty have provided certain organizational guidelines which, although flexible, are specifically structured to foster a correspondence between the membership and the objectives of the movement. Thus, for exam-

[23] Ralph H. Turner and Lewis M. Killian, *Collective Behavior* (Englewood Cliffs, N.J.: Prentice-Hall, 1957), p. 335.
[24] For a discussion of this phenomenon see David Danzig, "In Defense of Black Power," *Commentary,* September 1966, pp. 41–46.

ple, to qualify for participation in the movement, Community Action Programs must be developed in neighborhoods that meet certain criteria of poverty and the poor must be represented on the Community Action Agency's Board of Directors. These restrictions, of course, do not guarantee that members will be attracted to the movement or that those who do participate will actually represent a broad cross-section of the poverty population.

Group Identification. This phenomenon is associated, though not synonymous, with congruent membership. The latter is based upon social characteristics, whereas identification pertains to the attitudinal characteristics of a movement's members. To achieve solidarity, membership must not only correspond to the achievement of the movement's objectives, but the members must also broadly identify with the larger group that the movement represents, such as laborers, Negroes, women, farmers, or communists. Within any of these larger groups numerous points of identification exist. For instance, labor-movement members might identify with specific subgroups according to sex, race, occupation, or ethnic background. Narrow identification based upon these characteristics tends to split the movement, limit cooperation, and diminish its potential for effecting change.

In structuring congruent membershsip, one of the objectives of the War on Poverty is to facilitate broad identification with the abstract group that this movement represents. However, because of the stigma by which the poor are associated with an inferior species, this point of identification is not particularly appealing. "The disadvantaged" would have been a less opprobrious label, but was probably too long for political slogans and newspaper headlines. Other reform movements have been able to establish a socially legitimate sphere of identification: the civil rights advocate is attempting to realize the traditional American dream of equality and justice; the laborer is a hard-working productive member of the economic system; and the communist is seeking to create a classless society. But the poor are still, in many quarters, identified in Darwinian terms as the group simply incapable of independent survival. Thus the participants in the War on Poverty are, perhaps, prone to identify with more creditable subgroups based, for example, on racial, residential, or functional characteristics, rather than with the larger group that this movement represents.

Common Ideology. The term ideology is used here to represent a complex of ideas characteristic for a social movement. It is the core of values and beliefs that provide a rationale for both the objectives of the movement and the means for obtaining these objectives. A lack of consensus concerning these beliefs is likely to have a disruptive effect upon the movement.[25] A good example is provided by Henry Demarest Lloyd in his discussion of the demise of the People's Party in the late nineteenth century:

> No party can cohere unless its members have some common article of faith so completely engrained in the very texture of their minds that they spontaneously and without the necessity of conference will take practically the same views of the same question. The People's Party is a fortuitous collection of the dissatisfied. If it had been organized around a clearcut principle, of which its proposals were merely external expressions, it could never have been seduced into fusion. . . .[26]

One crucial aspect of the beliefs that constitute the ideology of most reform movements is the interpretation of the historical processes underlying the present state of affairs. In reference to the antipoverty ideology from a perspective of institutional malfunctioning, these beliefs are drawn from what Richard Hofstadter terms the "new psychology." Reflected in the ideas of such men as Veblen, Dewey, and Cooley, this school of thought interprets the phenomena of poverty not as consequences of the tooth-and-claw process of natural selection, but as a product of the institutional structure of society.

> The older psychology had been atomistic; Spencer for example, had seen society as the more or less automatic result of the char-

[25] For a discussion of the consequences of internal conflict over the ideas that form the basis of group consensus, see Lewis Coser, pp. 72–80.

[26] Caro Lloyd, *Henry Demarest Lloyd* (New York: Knickerbocker Press, 1912), Vol. 1, p. 263.

acters and instincts of its members; and this had given color to his conclusion that the improvement of society must be a slow evolutionary process waiting upon the gradual increment of personal characteristics "adapted" to the life conditions of modern industrial society. The new psychology, prepared to see the interdependence of the individual personality with the institutional structure of society, was destroying this one-way notion of social causation and criticizing its underlying individualism.[27]

Through this element of ideology runs the designation of an enemy —the group whose self-interests are tied to the maintenance of the present system of institutional arrangements. This system is often referred to as one of "welfare colonialism."[28] The "colonialists" are those with power who sanction, control, and plan programs for or (as the qualifications for public assistance and the results of urban renewal sometimes suggest) against the poor. This group constitutes the enemy: the ubiquitous "power structure."

This ideology of the antipoverty movement also extends to beliefs concerning the effects its program will have upon society. As Nathan Glazer indicates:

> Ideologically, the Community Action Program is based upon an analysis of what ails the poor. The analysis asserts that it is not their obvious material lack which is the heart of their problem. It is their lack of power. The vote does not give them power, because it needs education and money and time and social and organizational skills to organize the vote, and the poor do not have these. The imbalance is to be redressed by community organization. The effect, it is hoped, will be to improve education, welfare services, . . . and eventually, through increase in power, to change the pattern of rewards and services distributed by the public agencies.[29]

[27] Richard Hofstadter, *Social Darwinism in American Thought* (Boston: Beacon Press, 1962), p. 159.

[28] The expression "welfare colonialism" was popularized by Charles Silberman; see his *Crisis in Black and White* (New York: Random House, 1964).

[29] Nathan Glazer, "The Grand Design of the Poverty Program," *The New York Times Magazine*, February 27, 1966, p. 71. The idea of the poor as constituents of the welfare system is discussed by Frank Riessman in "The

Anatomy of a Professional Movement

Briefly, from the perspective of institutional performance, the ideological elements of the War on Poverty may be summarized in terms of the following beliefs: The poor are unable to influence the institutions that shape their lives. These institutions are insensitive to the needs of the poor. These institutions operate in ways that tend to perpetuate a sense of powerlessness in the poor. Through democratic processes these institutions may be changed. Strengthening the political power of the poor will allow them to participate more effectively in these democratic processes. This power may be strengthened through organization.

Embodied in these beliefs is the democratic conviction that the poor should be allowed to share in the decisions that affect their lives. The phrase "participatory democracy" is, perhaps, the best expression of this central value around which these ideological beliefs of the War on Poverty cohere. Solidarity, as described above, provides an indication of the internal strength of a social movement. The success of a movement in achieving its initial objectives is in part based upon pitting this strength against opposing forces emanating from the external environment.[30]

OPPOSITION

The degree of opposition that a movement evokes may be conceptualized as a function of the relationship between the ideological position of the movement's members and the ideological

New Antipoverty Ideology," *Poverty and Human Resources Abstracts,* 1966, *1*(4), 5–16.

[30] As Peter M. Blau indicates, goal displacement in the course of organization is not an inevitable fate of all reform movements. Rather, this phenomenon is linked to the degree of external opposition. Although the element of internal solidarity is not explicitly considered, in a brief review of a study of the Tennessee Valley Authority he notes that the plans for reform were obstructed by what might be termed, in light of the scheme presented above, as the inability to achieve "congruent membership"; that is, "As men with conservative views who represented vested interests and not the majority of people in the area were appointed to its Board of Directors, T.V.A.'s policies became increasingly conservative and removed from New Deal principles." See *Bureaucracy in Modern Society* (New York: Random House, 1963), pp. 91–100.

position of the members of the relevant external system, that system being composed of the institutions towards which the movement's efforts for change are directed. It is clear that there must be some ideological differences, however slight, between a movement and the external system; otherwise there would be little reason for the movement's existence. In seeking reform, a social movement is, to some extent, seeking to extend its ideology to supplement or replace the ideology of the external system. The manner in which the external system defines the movement's ideology will determine the movement's access to legitimate means for promoting its program in society.

As Ralph Turner and Lewis Killian suggest, the external system may classify movements according to three types: respectable, peculiar, and revolutionary. The respectable movement evokes little opposition. Its ideology is fundamentally consistent with that of the external system and generally emphasizes individual, rather than institutional, change. Movements aimed at social reform are most often classified as peculiar or revolutionary. A revolutionary movement evokes a high degree of opposition that is manifested in attempts by the external system to block access to legitimate means for promoting its program; for example, consider the treatment accorded the Communist party in the United States. A peculiar movement is one that evokes a moderate degree of opposition, generally in the form of ridicule and ostracism. Although its ideology is relatively consistent with that of the external system, the hierarchies of values are often not exactly parallel. This type of movement is allowed limited access to legitimate means for promoting its program.[31] According to this classification, the War on Poverty falls into the intermediate category, aptly labeled "peculiar." The ideology of the antipoverty movement is based upon the prevailing values of society, particularly those values relating to equal opportunity, self-help, realization of individual capacities, and the enhancement of democratic processes. Although the community-action arm of this movement emphasizes advancing certain social

[31] Turner and Killian, pp. 327–329.

values, such as participatory democracy, at the expense of others, such as social control, this emphasis does not exceed the bounds of traditionally acceptable modes of social action. Neither this emphasis nor the strength of the movement constitutes a revolutionary threat that would evoke violent opposition. However, those segments of society that hold the value of social control dear and that benefit from other values that this program is seeking to modify, do furnish a moderate degree of opposition to the antipoverty movement.

There are two avenues to reducing opposition. A movement may modify its ideology to make it more consistent with that of the external system. Here the price of obtaining legitimacy ultimately entails some alteration of objectives. For example, in the War on Poverty movement the ideological belief in participatory democracy could be deemphasized and the beliefs in social control and an individual's right to service elevated to new importance. This modification would constitute a shift from the reform objective of institutional change to the more traditional objective of individual change. The second approach to reducing opposition entails a formidable struggle with the external system. Initially, the call to battle would operate to intensify opposition. But if the movement were successful, opposition would finally diminish and the objectives would remain intact. In this situation the potential for success is to a large extent predicated upon the development and maintenance of a high degree of solidarity.

CHAPTER III

The Pittsburgh
Structure

It was not by accident that Pittsburgh became one of the first ten cities in the nation to be funded by the Office of Economic Opportunity for a Community Action Program (CAP). Months before the Economic Opportunity Act was passed, at a time when few people were aware that a federal assault on poverty was being planned, a small group of individuals from Pittsburgh were busily traveling back and forth to Washington seeking information, establishing connections, writing proposals, and promoting the CAP idea within their agencies and throughout the city. These were the architects of Pittsburgh's program. Some of the key members of this group were: Morton Coleman, Assistant Secretary for Manpower and Training to Mayor Barr of Pittsburgh and then part-time instructor at the University of Pittsburgh Graduate School of Social Work; Gerson Green, then Director of Community Development for Neighborhood Centers Association, a local settlement house; James Cunningham, then Associate Director of ACTION-Housing, Inc., a city-wide housing and community development organization; and Kiernan Stenson, then Urban Extension Worker for ACTION-Housing, Inc. All had received graduate degrees in social work from the University of Pittsburgh with the exception of Cunningham, who had extensive experience in community organization.

These men were not only professional associates, but were also personal friends with a great deal of mutual respect. Stenson, Coleman, and Green had, at an earlier point in their careers, worked together for Kingsley Association, a Pittsburgh settlement house. In recalling this experience, they modestly suggest that it was the best settlement-house staff in the nation—a statement which may approximate the truth, considering their later accomplishments. Cunningham came to Pittsburgh from Chicago, where he had been the head of the Independent Voters of Illinois and Director of the Hyde Park Community Conference. They were all tireless workers with lively minds; they engaged in a vigorous exchange of ideas and provided a high degree of mutual support at a time when both were necessary for launching the antipoverty movement in Pittsburgh. Philosophically, they championed the Jeffersonian notion of democracy. Cunningham in all probability reflects the position of the others in viewing a variety of local citizens' organizations as creative alternatives to town-hall democracy:

> The old-fashioned town-meeting method of making major governmental decisions is inadequate and impossible for the metrop-

43

olis. There are, however, creative modern alternatives which in part fulfill the function of the old town meeting and help the metropolis perform its mission of producing an environment of dignity for people. These alternatives give the average householder an opportunity to move outward from his home and family to participate directly in public decisions. Whether the householder takes advantage of such opportunity is up to him. The democratic spirit demands that man be free to participate or not participate, according to his own choosing.[1]

With this philosophy in mind, they set about the task of building Pittsburgh's antipoverty program.

LAYING THE GROUNDWORK

Starting around the early spring of 1964, these architects began to lay the groundwork; drafts of the pending legislation were circulated to welfare agencies and citizen groups; ideas were sought about the application of various titles of the Economic Opportunity Act to Pittsburgh. The War on Poverty and community action became increasingly a part of the welfare vocabulary. Within the span of a little over eight months these men, with the aid of a few others, particularly Bernard Olshansky, then Planning Director of the Health and Welfare Association, were able to sell the community-action program idea to Pittsburgh's welfare agencies, to muster strong local political support, and to produce the final antipoverty package that the Office of Economic Opportunity funded on November 23, 1964—a feat that reflects their ability and determination. However, able and determined men in various cities throughout the nation were struggling at the same time in similar endeavors. To understand Pittsburgh's success, the role of circumstance cannot be ignored. The architects provided the initiative, but it was the city's unique informal welfare structure, its public mode of action, and its political reaction that allowed for so immediate and positive a response.

With a population of approximately 600,000, Pittsburgh

[1] James V. Cunningham, *The Resurgent Neighborhood* (Notre Dame, Ind.: Fides Publishers, 1965), pp. 191–192.

44

The Pittsburgh Structure

ranks as the sixteenth largest city in the United States. In many respects it is an urban technician's dream—large enough to contain the diverse problems of a major urban area, yet small enough to grasp. Pittsburgh's size, as opposed to that of "super cities" such as New York or Los Angeles, makes a comprehensive network of informal relationships between welfare-related leaders at least a possibility. However, size is only a predisposing factor. For this network to develop, some stimulus is needed; it may arise spontaneously (for example, in the form of a race riot), or it may be a planned effort by some organization that consciously sets out to bring various welfare-related groups together around common areas of concern. The latter function is generally performed by local Health and Welfare councils; however, these organizations focus mostly upon the private welfare sector, and linkages with public-welfare-related agencies (such as those responsible for urban renewal, public housing, public assistance, education, and public safety) are usually tenuous.

The primary impetus for the development of a comprehensive network came to Pittsburgh in 1957 with the creation of AC-TION-Housing, Inc. This organization was established by the Allegheny Conference on Community Development, which in turn was inspired by the Mellon family, one of the wealthiest families in America and the most influential family in Pittsburgh. The Allegheny Conference is the acknowledged embodiment of the Pittsburgh "establishment." With the support of its influential board and a grant from Pittsburgh's Buhl Foundation in 1960, ACTION-Housing initiated a demonstration Neighborhood Urban Extension program in one of the city's poverty neighborhoods, Homewood-Brushton.

One of the central concepts around which the Neighborhood Urban Extension program was developed was the utilization of available resources: "All the private and governmental organizations serving people and reaching them directly—urban universities, schools, police departments, public health departments, welfare agencies, human relations organizations, settlement houses, churches, civic organizations—would be mobilized so that full use of their re-

45

sources would be made—and so they would develop to their fullest potential."[2] In the process of mobilizing these resources a network of informal relationships was created. Cunningham and Stenson, working for ACTION-Housing, played important roles in building this network. When the antipoverty program seemed imminent, Green, an active member of the local chapter of the National Association of Social Workers and a dynamic force in the local settlement-house association, helped to tie the system together from his angle. Others, such as Olshansky working out of the Health and Welfare Association, also contributed to the development of an informal welfare network.

One more linkage was necessary to mobilize Pittsburgh's welfare network for an assault on poverty—the all-important political connection between the city's welfare system and its municipal government, and through the latter, a connection to the federal government. Much of the credit for establishing this linkage goes to Coleman, whose position as Assistant Secretary to the Mayor was of particular consequence. Although Mayor Barr was favorably disposed towards the antipoverty program, the fact that he had on his staff an extremely capable individual whom he could trust and who was also intimately familiar with and respected by the local welfare system cannot be dismissed. Had a man of Coleman's stature not been around, it is dubious that the lines of communication between the political and welfare leaders would have been so direct, or that the cooperation and trust marking the Pittsburgh effort would have been so firm.

Thus, the speed and decisiveness with which Pittsburgh responded to the antipoverty movement reflect both the positive inclinations of the local political leaders and the comprehensive network of informal institutional and personal relationships that were ready and waiting to be utilized in the summer of 1964. The architects were on a first-name basis with almost every principal actor in Pittsburgh's political and social welfare systems.

[2] ACTION-Housing, Inc., *Urban Extension.* Proceedings of the Pittsburgh Urban Extension Conference, July 5–6, 1961 (Pittsburgh ACTION-Housing, Inc., 1962), pp. 87–88.

The Pittsburgh Structure

However, the story is not complete. To understand the climate in which the architects were building, some attempt must be made to understand the qualitative realm of public action. It is difficult, at best, to describe cities in terms of a mode of public action; yet in Pittsburgh a pattern emerges that is so visible and so consistent that it cannot be overlooked. It explains, in part, the fact that between 1960 and 1967 Pittsburgh was one of the few cities of its size in the nation not to suffer the agony of racial violence, even though the usual provocations existed—the ghettos, the shoot-first psychology of the police, and a school system that had become increasingly segregated.[3] It explains, in part, the relative success of the city's urban renewal programs and the lack of serious conflict between Negroes and the Board of Education. It also explains many specific incidents such as the one in 1966 when Mrs. Dorothy Richardson, the chairman of a newly formed "action" organization called Citizens Against Slum Housing, was allowed to speak at an "establishment" conference on urban housing held at the Pittsburgh Hilton Hotel; she received a standing ovation although she and dozens of others had "crashed" and picketed the conference only a few minutes previously. In Pittsburgh, public action is characterized by a pattern of formal cooptation.[4] As one sharp-eyed reporter notes in describing the city, "it seems to have a capacity for absorbing the Negro leadership in official positions within the Establishment."[5] However, in another statement, he adds a parenthetical qualification: "Negro leaders have access to the School Board and the superintendent, they serve on the school administration's ad-

[3] It was not until mid-1968, in the wake of Dr. Martin Luther King's assassination, that Pittsburgh suffered its first major racial disturbance, and cooptation of Negro leadership became more difficult to achieve.

[4] Philip Selznick suggests that formal cooptation is most often utilized to establish the legitimacy of authority, and is not necessarily oriented toward a sharing of power. He hypothesizes that cooptation that results in the sharing of power tends to operate informally. See "Cooptation: A Mechanism for Organizational Stability," *Reader in Bureaucracy,* ed. Robert K. Merton and others (New York: Free Press, 1960), pp. 135–139.

[5] Peter Schrag, "Pittsburgh: The Virtues of Candor," *Saturday Review,* November 19, 1966, p. 84.

visory committee, and they are frequently consulted (if not heeded) on policy decisions."[6]

In setting out to build an antipoverty movement in Pittsburgh, the architects were thus starting on quite solid ground. Their talents and skills were applied to a city in which the lines of communication were fairly well established, the political system offered support, and the mode of public action, to a great extent, minimized the possibility of strong opposition.

CREATING THE STRUCTURE

In the mid-spring of 1964, at the request of Mayor Barr, a War on Poverty Planning Committee began to meet regularly in the Mayor's conference chambers at city hall. The committee was composed primarily of professionals representing the local public and private-welfare-related agencies. Initially it was made up of Charles H. Hayes, Director of Team Teaching, Pittsburgh Board of Education; John Cicco, Administrative Assistant to the Superintendent of Schools, Catholic Diocese of Pittsburgh; Norman Taylor, Senior Planner, Department of City Planning; Hugh B. Robins, District Health Officer, Allegheny County Health Department; George P. Mills, Executive Director of the Allegheny County Board of Public Assistance; Bernard Olshansky; James Cunningham; Morton Coleman; and, from time to time, Aldo Colautti, Mayor Barr's Executive Secretary. Shortly after the committee was formed, Kiernan Stenson and Gerson Green also became regularly attending members. The group had little formal structure, and other persons moved in and out as various issues arose. Coleman was assigned out of the mayor's office to work full time on the War on Poverty Program and, through a general consensus, became the chairman of this group.

During the period in which the Planning Committee operated, a number of decisions were made—some explicit and others implicit—that had long-range implications for the Pittsburgh structure. In reviewing these decisions, it is important to understand the

---

[6] Schrag, p. 83.

climate in which the group worked and the orientation of its members. Most of those who attended these meetings came from service-oriented programs and agencies. With the exception of the AC-TION-Housing staff and a few others, the participants' professional training and experience in program development was that of planning for the poor. The atmosphere in which the group met was infused with a sense of urgency; as one member notes, the feeling was that "if Pittsburgh didn't move quickly, and with some assurance of what was to be done, the much sought after OEO money would escape us and be directed to other cities."[7]

Service Orientation and Citizen Participation. One of the earliest and most important decisions concerning the Pittsburgh program was implicitly arrived at mainly through the very composition of the Planning Committee itself. That is, rather than attempting to develop a parallel structure of welfare services, the planners of the Pittsburgh program decided to utilize the currently available resources represented by the various members of the committee. In part, this decision reflected the urban-extension philosophy of ACTION-Housing, which in many ways provided a model for the emerging structure. But on its own merits, the idea to involve local agencies was, under the circumstances, a strategic maneuver; if time was of the essence, the price of the delay that would be involved in developing new agencies was too high to pay. Also, a parallel structure would provide a strong potential for conflict with the existing service system, and, as noted earlier, fostering this type of development was not consistent with the city's public mode of operation.

Citizen involvement in the planning effort was, at best, sporadic and of minor consequence. In neighborhoods such as Homewood-Brushton and Hazelwood-Glenwood, where, through the earlier organizing efforts of ACTION-Housing, strong citizens' councils existed, meetings were held to discuss and analyze the antipoverty legislation. But here again the pressure of time weighed

[7] Robert B. Williams, "Politics and Poverty," Paper read before a faculty meeting at the Carnegie Institute of Technology, Pittsburgh, February 16, 1967, p. 2.

49

heavily; in Hazelwood, for example, the time allotted for this process was two weeks. The organizer working in this neighborhood indicated that "to explain a very complicated, bureaucratically worded, nine-title piece of federal legislation to groups of neighborhood people who were basically unfamiliar with and unresponsive to any formal types of organization within a two-week period of time was not, in my opinion, an honest effort at involving citizens in planning of the program."[8] Other attempts were made to involve citizens; for example, Cunningham and Coleman, along with other members of the Planning Committee, asked one of the citizen leaders in the North Side to bring together a group of local youth. At the meeting of these youth, the problems of the neighborhood were discussed and the youth asked about services that the poverty program might provide to improve the local situation.

A few members of the Planning Committee were dissatisfied with these sporadic attempts to involve citizens, feeling that the citizens should have been present at the committee meetings at which the real decisions were made. When the proposals that were soon to constitute the official Pittsburgh program were finally completed, one of these members raised the issue of allowing the citizens to review the package before it was submitted to Washington for funding. This issue was brought to a vote, and an overwhelming majority of the members present opted to send the proposals directly to Washington. The Planning Committee was eager for Pittsburgh to get its share, or perhaps more than its share, of the federal largesse; there would be time for citizen participation after the funds were assured and the programs operating.

These decisions had significant implications for the Pittsburgh program. They established a service orientation that was to continue through 1966, when the federal antipoverty budget began to be cut back. During this period, money and manpower were largely devoted to providing coordinated services to the poor, with a strong emphasis upon education. This orientation did not explicitly discount the importance of citizen involvement; it was sim-

[8] Williams, p. 2.

50

ply relegated to second place. The decision-makers in Pittsburgh were responding to Washington's call for immediate action. For this response they were summarily rewarded. The program was initially funded in 1964 for approximately $1.5 million. In the following fiscal year, 1965–1966, Pittsburgh was one of the first cities to have its program refunded; and this time the OEO grant was for $7.3 million (although only $6.8 million was eventually spent).

Immediate action meant the establishment of an organization that could spend money, build programs, and produce concrete results without upsetting the applecart of local politics; the quality and relevance of these results were, at that stage, of secondary importance. In addition to the external pressure for action, there were the internal pressures upon the new organization to advertise its existence and to establish its credibility. What better way was there to gain the confidence of local agencies than by involving them in the development and operation of service programs for which the Community Action Agency would provide 90 per cent of the funds? Also, when considering all the accouterments necessary for service programs—such as physical locus, staff, intake forms, and files—it is obvious that this approach served the secondary function of providing visibility and concreteness for the new organization.

A program centering upon the development of citizen participation does not meet the criteria of immediate action, credibility, visibility, and concreteness. On the contrary, the development of such a program involves a prolonged and elusive process, the results of which are difficult to gauge. It is rarely concrete enough, for instance, to enable one to specify the number of clients served per month. Participation-oriented programs are politically volatile and often achieve visibility in the act of disturbing the status quo. This places the sponsoring organization in a weak position to capture the confidence of local agencies. Thus, in the initial stage of creating the Pittsburgh Community Action Agency structure, the decision-makers responded to both internal and external pressures that weighed in favor of allocating resources to provide services to the poor rather than to stimulate citizen involvement. This course of action was not a conscious conspiracy to keep the poor quiet and maintain the status quo; it was a compromise which allowed the Community Action Agency to become established and to expand within an exceedingly short period of time.

However, stressing service did not mean totally ignoring citizen participation. As reflected in the Planning Committee's policy statement concerning the structure and role of citizens' groups, there was still a very strong commitment to involving citizens in a decision-making capacity once the program was under way. This policy called for citizens' groups to help plan and review all proposals for programs to be carried out in the neighborhoods as well as to evaluate programs once they were put into operation. These citizens' groups were to be the official representatives of the Community Action Agency at the neighborhood level and were to be consulted prior to the Community Action Agency's renewal of delegate agency contracts. Delegate agencies were the social welfare organizations that the Community Action Agency funded to provide neighborhood services. In addition, citizens' groups were slated to play an important part in the recruitment, screening, and final selection of key neighborhood staff.

Organizational Structure. Another cornerstone decision in the development of the Pittsburgh antipoverty program concerned the structure of the Community Action Agency. There were three broad alternatives: establishing a city agency, a quasi-public body, or a private nonprofit corporation. A number of considerations militated against the creation of a public or quasi-public agency. The objections to a public agency centered around three issues: (a)' First was the potential for conflict and resistance inherent in a structure that would involve coordination of interjurisdictional public bodies by a city agency—the Health Department is a county agency; the Department of Public Assistance is run by a county board using state and federal funds; the Bureau of Employment Security is a state agency; and the Board of Public Education is appointed by the courts and has its own taxing power. (b) Next was the concern for the quality and independence of staff—the Planning Committee recognized the limitations that the salary scale and political pressures of public municipal employment would impose on the attraction and operation of the aggressive, innovative, free-wheeling staff they wanted for the new enterprise. (c) Finally, there was the considerable risk that the program might be a bomb of some sort, and a public agency is particularly vulnerable to attack—the mayor had no desire to absorb the political shock waves within the four walls of his office.

The creation of a quasi-public body was a somewhat more palatable idea, particularly in light of the successful experience with Pittsburgh's Urban Redevelopment Authority. This alternative offered a more indirect and less stringent form of political control, by way of the requirement to work through the city council and the careful appointment of board members. It also eliminated the problem of staff salaries being tied to the city pay scale. But the isolation of staff from political pressures was an important criterion for the Planning Committee, one which could be more readily accomplished through a private nonprofit corporation. Compared to an authority, the creation of a nonprofit corporation involved a less time-consuming and less complex legal process. And, by involving a wide range of powerful interests on the board of this corporation, the mayor would have a buffer to help absorb any negative repercussions that might arise. Thus, the Planning Committee settled upon creating, as Pittsburgh's official Community Action Agency, the Mayor's Committee on Human Resources, Inc. (MCHR), a private nonprofit corporation with the mayor as Chairman of the Board of Directors. This alternative placed the new antipoverty organization outside the realm of the formal political structure and at the same time allowed the mayor to maintain a more than nominal degree of control over its administration.

Target Neighborhoods. The Planning Committee wanted Pittsburgh's program to cover as many of the poverty areas in the city as possible. As a guide to the selection of these areas, an Urban Level-of-Living Index, prepared by the Health and Welfare Association for the Department of City Planning, was utilized. This index provided a figure for each census tract in Pittsburgh, based upon the following criteria: income, education, employment, home

53

ownership, housing conditions, public assistance, and juvenile delinquency. These figures showed a wide geographic distribution of poverty throughout the city.

The problem then was how to organize the numerous census tracts so as to cover the most ground while at the same time maintaining a feasible administrative ratio with the Community Action Agency. The Planning Committee considered eight or nine neighborhood units to be about the numerical limit that the MCHR could effectively coordinate, but the Index showed more than twice this number of impoverished neighborhoods. The solution was to select eight areas with loose boundaries based upon a tractile concept of "neighborhood." Thus, whereas South Oakland is a fairly distinct neighborhood in the sense that it is identified as such by the residents and is geographically compact, the North Side is actually an intermixture of at least four somewhat distinct neighborhoods, Central North Side, East North Side, Manchester, and North View Heights; and Southwest is really composed of four geographically separate sections, each of which contains at least one and in some cases two neighborhoods of its own.

The eight areas were ranked in order of need, somehow based upon the data in Table 1. However, the exact formula for this priority ranking was never made clear (seemingly because there was none), nor were the implications of these priorities ever specified beyond the general understanding that the high-ranking neighborhoods were entitled to greater consideration in the allocation of antipoverty resources. Because of this vagueness, the priorities were, from the very beginning of the program, a bone of contention; for example, the largest neighborhoods (Southwest and North Side) claimed that the priorities should be reordered to reflect better the overall quantitative needs of each area, which obviously were greater in these areas because of their population size.

Coordinating Agencies. With the general target areas agreed upon, the next important issue tackled by the Planning Committee was the structure of neighborhood coordination. Coordination was a vitally strategic function in the proposed antipoverty effort. The neighborhood coordinator would be responsible for

FIGURE 1. PITTSBURGH'S ANTIPOVERTY NEIGHBORHOODS

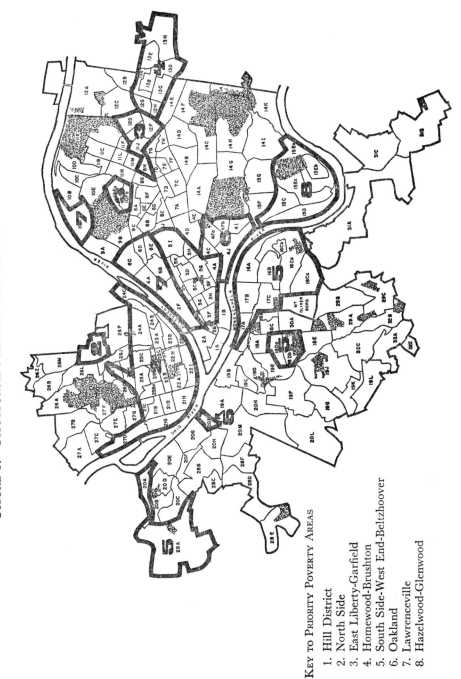

KEY TO PRIORITY POVERTY AREAS

1. Hill District
2. North Side
3. East Liberty-Garfield
4. Homewood-Brushton
5. South Side-West End-Beltzhoover
6. Oakland
7. Lawrenceville
8. Hazelwood-Glenwood

Table 1

POVERTY NEIGHBORHOOD STATISTICS

Neighborhoods[a]	Median Family Income, 1959	Median Years of Completed Education, 25 or over, 1960	Percentage of Male Labor Force Unemployed, 1960	Percentage of Defective Housing, 1960	Percentage of Public Assistance Recipients, 1965	Total Population, 1960
Hill District	$3,893	9.2	19.4	43	31.4	37,219
North Side	$4,871	8.7	14.9	57.5	17.0	64,949
East Liberty-Garfield	$4,638	9.5	12.7	48.5	16.5	21,465
Homewood-Brushton	$4,627	9.8	10.5	44.5	21.4	30,732
Southwest Pittsburgh	$4,857	9.4	10.1	31.65	11.48	50,008
South Oakland	$5,033	10.2	9.7	34.2	8.6	16,904
Lawrenceville	$5,657	9.0	9.1	41.6	10.6	17,435
Hazelwood-Glenwood	$4,849	9.3	7.5	21.4	13.9	17,308

[a] Neighborhoods are listed in order of priority, as determined by need.

56

organizing and staffing local citizens' groups and for insuring the systematic delivery of local welfare services. The initial thought of the Committee was that this function should be delegated to AC-TION-Housing, primarily because of its experience in conducting the Neighborhood Urban Extension program, which was providing a model for Pittsburgh's community-action efforts. Although it does not appear that ACTION-Housing actively sought to influence this decision, the agency was not averse to accepting it. However, some planners opposed this structure, particularly Gerson Green, who aggressively stimulated the neighborhood settlement houses to defend their interests. Representing this group before the Planning Committee, he put forth a forcible argument against centralizing the coordination function under one agency, an argument which was strongly supported by Morton Coleman. They favored a decentralized system of coordination, by settlement houses in four of the poverty neighborhoods and by ACTION-Housing in the other four (where there were either no settlement houses or where the existing settlement houses were recreation-oriented with no community-organization components).

Theoretically, decentralization was advantageous insofar as it would allow for greater flexibility and innovation, two principles to which the Planning Committee was pledged. However, when applied to Pittsburgh, this argument stretched credibility somewhat. In the area of community development, innovation and flexibility were hardly the right terms to describe the past performance of the local settlement houses. Indeed, if past performance was any indication of future results, then ACTION-Housing led the field. Other less clearly articulated considerations perhaps carried more weight. AC-TION-Housing was, for many reasons, suspect. For example, its board represented some of the most powerful interests in the city, a fact its detractors saw as evidence that the agency was an "establishment tool"; its public relations department was particularly expansive and aggressive, frequently tending to exaggerate the agency's successes while disclaiming its failures. Still, the agency was not afraid of innovation, and the results, if not always as sparkling as claimed, were often impressive when compared to other efforts at community development in Pittsburgh. However, regardless of the agency's actual accomplishments, its detractors imputed fraudulent motives and frequently based their criticisms more on this allegation than on tangible factors.

Also to be considered in the argument against centralization was the fact that most of the settlement houses bidding for coordination contracts were well entrenched in their neighborhoods; placing the coordinating function under ACTION-Housing would upset the status quo, create a dual system of community development within each neighborhood, and undoubtedly evoke a power struggle in some of the areas. Furthermore, it was conceivable that under this centralized system, ACTION-Housing would emerge as a powerful threat to the MCHR itself. Thus, the Planning Committee finally decided to divide the coordination function between the settlement houses and ACTION-Housing. The contracts for this service were allocated as follows:

ACTION-Housing	Homewood-Brushton
	Hazelwood-Glenwood
	Lawrenceville
	South Oakland
Hill House Association	Hill District
Neighborhood Centers Association	North Side
Kingsley Association	East Liberty-Garfield
Brashear Association	Southwest Pittsburgh

Community Action Agency Board of Directors. The final task of the Planning Committee was the establishment of guidelines for the selection of the Community Action Agency's Board of Directors. These guidelines, following the OEO model, recommended that the Mayor's Committee on Human Resources, Inc. Board be composed, in the main, of executive members of the boards of directors of key welfare-related organizations. As these positions are usually held by individuals representing the city's dominant power groups, it was envisioned that the MCHR Board would serve a dual function by opening two lines of communication. That is, the board members would provide formal linkages with the local welfare system and informal linkages with powerful social, economic, and political institutions.

Following these guidelines, the mayor's staff initially selected ten members to serve on the MCHR Board: Mayor Joseph M. Barr; Bishop Vincent M. Leonard, Vicar-General of the Catholic Diocese of Pittsburgh; Mr. William P. Young, State Secretary of Labor and Industry; Judge David Olbum, head of the City Planning Board; Patrick T. Fagan, President of City Council; Robert Ferguson, head of the Health and Welfare Board; Howard Hague, Vice-President of the United Steel Workers of America; Byrd Brown, President of the Pittsburgh NAACP; William H. Rea, head of the Pittsburgh Board of Public Education; and J. Stanley Purnell, head of the ACTION-Housing, Inc. Board. On October 2, 1964, the Planning Committee, after reviewing this list, recommended that the membership be expanded to include representation of neighborhood people and additional representation of the Negro community. A few weeks later part of this recommendation received a strong boost when the Ad Hoc Group in Relation to the Antipoverty Program, a committee composed of Pittsburgh's Negro leadership, submitted a memorandum to Mayor Barr calling for, among other things, greater representation of Negroes on the MCHR Board.

In response to the demands of the Ad Hoc Group and the recommendations of the Planning Committee, the board of directors was expanded to include three additional Negro representatives chosen from a list that the Ad Hoc Group had submitted to the mayor's office. The three new members came from neighborhoods ranking first, second, and fourth on the antipoverty priority list. They were: Frankie Pace, Vice-President of the Citizens for Hill District Renewal; James J. Robinson, a minister from the North Side; and J. A. Williams, a minister from Homewood-Brushton. In a last-minute addition, Robert Pease, Director of the Urban Redevelopment Authority, was also selected to serve on the board; he was included primarily because of local and federal desires for a close link between antipoverty and urban renewal activities.

On November 23, 1964, the Mayor's Committee on Human

Clients or Constituents

Resources, Inc. officially came into existence. Its board was composed of fourteen members representing a wide range of interests. However, the poor as a group were not formally and directly represented in this body, and neither were the neighborhoods. Although some of the board members actually did reside in poverty neighborhoods, they were either hand-picked by the mayor or chosen from the lists submitted by the Ad Hoc Group; and the latter were selected more as representatives-at-large of the Negro community than as neighborhood representatives or representatives of the poor in general. At no time were the neighborhood citizens' councils consulted about these choices.

As the MCHR began operations, this absence of low-income representatives started to draw criticism from residents and staff in the neighborhoods. Also, the board members themselves recognized that the requirements for "maximum feasible participation" of the poor included representation in policy-making positions. On July 2, 1965, the issue of expanding board membership was again opened for discussion. The initial thoughts of MCHR's members were that two or three low-income members should be added to the board as delegates-at-large. The reasoning was that the delegate-at-large structure, as opposed to geographic representation, would facilitate rising above the "neighborhood-point-of-view" and allow the low-income members to consider policy issues in terms of broader implications.[9] This structure was also seen as providing a counterbalance to the parochialism that characterized neighborhood-council planning efforts.

On November 5, 1965, a subcommittee chaired by Judge Olbum was appointed by the board to explore alternatives for expanding the membership. Shortly afterwards, this subcommittee met with the presidents of the eight neighborhood councils to discuss the issue. From this meeting emerged the recommendation that seven low-income persons be chosen for the board without regard to neighborhood distribution. However, after subsequent subcom-

[9] Minutes of the Board of Directors Meeting, July, 2, 1965, Mayor's Committee on Human Resources, Inc. (in the files of the MCHR).

60

mittee meetings with neighborhood citizens' councils, this recommendation was altered in line with the councils' recommendation; the citizens' councils wanted eight neighborhood representatives, to be selected by the MCHR from a list prepared separately in each neighborhood. Although this procedure would eliminate a representative-at-large structure, Judge Olbum observed that, under the circumstances, attempts to develop such a structure would likely create friction between the MCHR and the neighborhood councils.[10] On January 28, 1966, the MCHR voted to accept this revised recommendation. It took four more months to complete the selection process and install the new members. Thus it took a total of about eighteen months, from the time the MCHR came into existence until the spring of 1967, for the poor to get into the policy-making chambers of Pittsburgh's War on Poverty.

SELECTING STAFF

With the newly formed agency in existence, the first task of the MCHR Board was to obtain an executive director. In November of 1964, a Personnel Selection Committee was appointed—composed of Byrd Brown, William Rea, Rev. J. A. Williams, Robert Pease, and Aldo Colautti (not a board member but representing the mayor)—to interview applicants for this position. Although the organization would be operating in problem areas closely related to social work and education, the Committee did not consider professional credentials in these fields as necessary prerequisites for the position. On the contrary, it was thought that such professionals might tend to view the problems from too technical a perspective, in contrast to an administrative generalist capable of operating with a broad view. In this respect the executive director's position presented a typical case of institutionalized role conflict.[11] On the one hand, the job called for a professional social worker or educator to insure that the executive's commitments and ex-

[10] Minutes of the Board of Directors Meeting, January 28, 1966, Mayor's Committee on Human Resources, Inc. (in the files of the MCHR).

[11] Amitai Etzioni, *Modern Organizations* (Englewood Cliffs, N.J.: Prentice-Hall, 1964), pp. 75–93.

61

pertise would be congruent with the organization's welfare-related goals and that the needs of the organization's professional staff would receive due recognition. On the other hand, this position required certain skills that were only indirectly related to specific organizational goals and professional activities; the ability, for example, to obtain federal monies, to recruit personnel, and to allocate funds to delegate agencies was crucial to the maintenance and expansion of the MCHR. It appears that the committee thought that a social worker or an educator might overemphasize primary goal activities to the neglect of these administrative functions.

Although this view is valid to the extent that social workers and educators are in general likely to stress technical and programmatic factors more than administrative considerations, there are numerous exceptions. Of those who applied for the executive director's position in Pittsburgh, at least three social workers were more than capable of exacting an operational balance between the professional and administrative spheres, as attested to by past experience and subsequent events; one later became deputy director of ACTION-Housing, another went to a high administrative post in the Office of Economic Opportunity, and the third was appointed dean of a graduate school of social work.

Another factor also had to be considered in making this selection—the factor of race. Here again the Ad Hoc Group tried to exert influence; in addition to pressing for Negro representation on the MCHR Board, the Ad Hoc Group also sought to have Negroes hired into the top administrative posts. Initially, there were to be four such high-level positions: executive director, director of operations, assistant director of operations, and director of research and evaluation. The Ad Hoc Group especially wanted a Negro for the executive director's slot; but, if a qualified person could not be found, their alternative was to have Negroes selected for the two operations positions. They were least interested in the director of research and evaluation because it was thought that, of the four positions, this one offered the least in terms of influencing policy or program implementation.

The Pittsburgh Structure

It is difficult to determine how much bearing the Ad Hoc Group's demands had upon the Personnel Selection Committee's decisions. In a society in which the idea of equal opportunity is cherished, at least in the abstract, preferential treatment for Negroes is a sensitive issue; as such, it may be practiced, but it is rarely preached. However, whether the Committee was responding primarily to the Ad Hoc Group's demands or to its own inclinations, it is clear that in recruiting for an executive director they sought an individual with broad administrative experience who was preferably a Negro. By January 1965, they had narrowed down the field of applicants to six individuals. Racially, this group was composed of three Negroes and three whites; in terms of their backgrounds, there were four social workers, one administrator with a political science background, and one lawyer. It was the lawyer, David Hill, who was finally chosen for the position of executive director. Prior to this, Hill had served for three and one-half years as an assistant United States attorney for the Western District of Pennsylvania, directing a staff of seven people. This experience, although not vast, along with the fact of his race (Negro) and his childhood experience with poverty and life in Pittsburgh's major ghetto (Hill District), weighed heavily in favor of Hill's selection.

ORGANIZING NEIGHBORHOODS

When the Community Action Program was launched in the winter of 1965, the problem of creating neighborhood-citizen structures was already partly solved. In six of the eight target neighborhoods, citizens' councils were already in existence. These councils varied with regard to sophistication, level of activity, age, organizational stability, and representativeness. Some, such as the Kingsley Neighborhood Association in East Liberty, had been in operation for a number of years and maintained a stable but low level of activity, rarely causing any excitement within or beyond the area. Others were like the Central North Side Neighborhood Council, which had a very erratic pattern of activity, coming to life as crises arose and subsequently fading back into a state of near inactivity. Also, there were a few, particularly the councils representing Home-

63

wood-Brushton and Hazelwood-Glenwood, that had maintained a fairly high level of activity over an extended period of time. These latter two had the most experience in mobilizing local people and resources, and in this sense were best prepared to operate within the context of the antipoverty program.

Because of this variation, three different procedures were employed to develop the neighborhood council structures: consolidation, expansion, and organization. The first two procedures were utilized in the six neighborhoods where one or more citizens' organizations already existed. Rather than attempting to organize totally new structures in these areas, the approach was to bring together the existing groups, or representatives thereof, to form one council that would be officially recognized by the MCHR as representing the entire neighborhood; in most instances, membership on these councils had to be expanded to meet the MCHR requirements concerning representation of the poor. In Lawrenceville and South Oakland, the two neighborhoods that had no citizens groups, it was necessary for the coordinating agency, ACTION-Housing, to undertake basic organizational activities.

Ultimately, eight citizens' councils were developed and recognized by the MCHR as representing the antipoverty neighborhoods. Ordered according to neighborhood priority, they are: Hill District Citizens Committee on Economic Opportunity, North Side Committee on Human Resources, East Liberty-Garfield Citizens Advisory Committee, Homewood-Brushton Citizens Renewal Council, Citizens Board of Southwest Pittsburgh, South Oakland Citizens Council, Lawrenceville Economic Action Program, Hazelwood-Glenwood Glen Hazel Extension Council. The variety of names by which these councils chose to identify themselves is significant, in that it reflects the strong mark of individuality that characterized neighborhood participation in Pittsburgh's antipoverty movement; these names barely suggest the fact that all eight groups were partners in the same program.

To a lesser extent, differences also existed in the council structures. In the North Side and the Hill District, the councils had two levels of participation: general membership and executive officers. The general membership, consisting of all citizens wishing to participate, was considered as the council's board of directors, and they elected the executive officers. This structure allowed the general membership a direct role in making council policy. The other six neighborhood councils had three levels of participation: general membership, board of directors, and executive committee of the board. Here the boards of directors were "elected" by the general membership or (in at least one case) appointed by the director of the coordinating agency, and the boards subsequently elected their own executive officers; these boards ranged in membership from thirty to sixty people and were responsible for making council policy. In Chapter VIII the processes by which board members were chosen are discussed in greater detail, particularly their implications for representativeness.

In developing these neighborhood boards, a mixture of inducements was used to motivate citizens to participate. First, there were inducements through status appeal. For example, an appeal to status desires was implicit when potential board members were approached by the director of a coordinating agency or by the neighborhood organizer; the fact that these boards were to receive official recognition from the mayor also imparted status to membership; and, perhaps most significant in this respect was the notion that the boards represented the "cream" of the local populace, and that, as groups, they would supposedly be vested with serious responsibilities and powers. The second inducement was the "newistic" attraction. The Community Action Program was widely acclaimed as a "new" approach to solving the ills of poverty. It was to be a coordinated, comprehensive, and decentralized attack—reaching the very core of the neighborhood by involving the poor in the planning and the delivery of needed services. The use of specious claims in the promotion of a new product or idea has, through modern advertising, become so pervasive as to effect an almost Pavlovian reflex. Like the sound of Pavlov's bell, the establishment of a product or idea as new has in itself become enough of a stimulant; the claims themselves are no longer really necessary. For example, "a *new* taste in cigarettes" is without difficulty substituted for "a *great* taste in a new cigarette." Although the official claims made for the antipoverty program were not extravagant, the emphasis on a "new" innovative approach attracted many people, particularly those who had lived through the frustrating experience of participation on the "old" councils.[12]

The third factor that fostered participation was socioeconomic discontent, which the organizers themselves often helped to stimulate. This technique is frequently identified with the conflict school of community organization, most probably because a fomenter of discontent is usually termed an agitator, and an agitator implies conflict. But, as the Pittsburgh program clearly illustrates, there is no necessary connection between the stimulation of discontent and the conflict approach to problem-solving. It all depends upon what problems are presented and how they are presented, particularly the emotional tenor and the interpretation of causes. In organizing the neighborhoods, one means of stimulating discontent was by getting people to verbalize their problems. When the Lawrenceville Council was being organized, the citizens were asked one question at almost every meeting: "What do you consider to be the most pressing problems in your neighborhood?" Another approach was the presentation of the objective reality, or the facts, to the citizens; at the meetings in Lawrenceville the organizing staff frequently distributed a simple fact sheet that told the story of dependency, poor health, juvenile delinquency, unemployment, and miseducation in the neighborhood.

Although status appeal, the "newistic" attraction, and socioeconomic discontent partly explain individual participation on neighborhood boards, another motivating factor was quite influential. Aside from supplying services, the antipoverty program promised a number of nonprofessional jobs to residents, and many citizens quickly realized that these jobs would go to those who were familiar with the program and active in the community, and that the board members, besides having these qualities, would be among

[12] A further analysis of the "newistic" attraction and its application to reform movements is presented by Joseph W. Eaton, *Stone Walls Not a Prison Make* (Springfield, Ill.: Thomas, 1962), pp. 35–38.

the first people in the neighborhood to learn about these jobs. Thus, for some (and probably many), participation was viewed primarily as the most direct route to employment.

IMPLICATIONS OF STRUCTURE

In viewing the development of Pittsburgh's program, it is abundantly clear that the poor had little influence upon creating the structure in which they would participate; decisions ranging from the number of target neighborhoods to the composition of the MCHR were made, essentially, by a small group of welfare professionals and political aides.

Did these professionals create a structure that would facilitate the reformist objective of the antipoverty movement—to allow the poor greater influence over decisions that affect their lives? Was the structure one that would foster the solidarity necessary to accomplish this objective? Was it one that would evoke opposition? In answer to these questions, a number of points, summarized below, suggest that the structure created in Pittsburgh was one which, while inhibiting opposition, at the same time inhibited the potential for radical action. To begin with, the early decisions concerning Pittsburgh's antipoverty structure were weighted heavily in favor of preserving the status quo; funds were allocated primarily for the expansion of services utilizing existing agencies; and community organization staff, who had the greatest and perhaps only potential for creating strong pressures for change, were held to a bare minimum. Citizens' influence was restricted by the very fact that citizens first gained representation on the MCHR Board sixteen months after the program was funded—by which time its course was fairly well charted. Moreover, when the citizens were allowed to participate on the board, they came not as representatives of the poor, but as representatives of geographic areas; this supported a neighborhood orientation that, in turn, hindered the development of solidarity.

Another constraint to building solidarity was the racial identification established at the beginning of the program. When the MCHR Board was first formed, it contained agency representatives and three representatives of the Negro community, whereas the antipoverty movement was supposed to be aimed at the poor, both black and white. This representational structure tended to identify it as a Negro program, as a new branch of the civil rights movement. This identification was reinforced by the quite obvious preference for hiring a Negro director and large numbers of Negro staff at all levels.

Finally, dividing the coordination function among five different agencies reinforced the neighborhood as a reference point for identification and reduced the possibility of linking neighborhoods together in a city-wide effort. In attempting to maintain the status quo by allowing each agency to coordinate the neighborhood that was already under its "sphere of influence," little thought was given to alternative structures that might have strengthened citizen participation. For instance, the idea of contracting for coordination directly with citizens' groups was barely explored. Although most of the citizens' groups were probably not ready to shoulder this responsibility, there was still the possibility, for example, of placing the coordination function under the MCHR directly, with the understanding that control would be transferred to the citizens within a specified period of time.

Just described are some of the major efforts that went into molding Pittsburgh's structure—efforts exerted primarily by professionals. The interrelationship between the professionals and the structure must be viewed from a different perspective, for the structure, once in operation, imposed certain limitations and constraints upon professional functioning.

CHAPTER IV

The Professional Organizers

Eight neighborhood coordinators, with their respective staffs of two to six assistant coordinators, work out of Pittsburgh's eight target areas. These individuals come from varied backgrounds: four were experienced social workers, two were public housing administrators, one was a Peace Corps volunteer, and one was an editor of a community newspaper. All have college degrees, and none live in the neighborhoods in which they work. Thus, they are "outsiders" in almost every sense.

These coordinators have two key qualities in common: a stamina that allows them to work about sixty hours a week, and a temperament that permits them to function under conditions of "chaotic ambiguity." This ambiguity is reflected even in the title "coordinator." The verb "coordinate" is variously defined as meaning to equalize, to harmonize, to adjust, or to organize; and the coordinator is expected to fulfill all four functions—organizing the citizens, adjusting the service system, harmonizing the relationships between citizens' groups and between citizens and agencies, and equalizing the opportunity for citizens to participate in community decision-making. These tasks are, obviously, not always congruent; often, choices must be made between them, as between harmony and equality; and, in making this type of choice, there are no established guidelines to follow and no clear set of priorities. The chaotic dimension of this position is largely manifest in the day-to-day crises that emerge in working with the poor. For example, many cases of individual problems come to the attention of the coordinator; although some may be handled by referral (to one of the service components in the neighborhood center), others require immediate and personal assistance. The coordinator must frequently take the initiative and the time to obtain anything from a bus to a bed, to find shelter for an evicted tenant, or to have the heat turned on in a client's home.

The work generates considerable pressures: night meetings, take-home work, and Saturdays at the office leave little time for family life and other relaxation. An experience related by Bob Ruffin, former Northside Coordinator, illustrates the pervasiveness of the job. After working at it for almost two years, he finally planned a quiet vacation at home with his family. During the first few days the quiet was shattered by the constant ringing of the telephone—staff and citizens calling to discuss problems, to seek advice, and to obtain information; there were also obligatory evening meetings to attend. Realizing that he had left the office but not the job, he cut the "vacation" short and returned to the office. Bob Ruffin's experience was not an uncommon one. Of the eight coordinators initially hired, five were still on the job two years later.

Bob Williams, a former Bostonian and Peace Corps volunteer, is one of the best men on the job. Having come to Pittsburgh in 1963 as an urban extension worker for ACTION-Housing, he holds seniority with four years at the "grass roots" level; at thirty-two he is graying at the temples. As an organizer, Williams has a rough, colorful, and distinctive style; sometimes he talks, Bogart-style, out of the side of his mouth, uses direct language, and is not above employing moderate profanities or banging his fist on the table to drive home a point. However, Bob Williams will sooner or later move out of the grass roots, probably into a less taxing administrative position downtown. Few coordinators will match even his four years at the job.

SELECTION PROCESS

The selection of neighborhood coordinators was a sensitive process. The citizens, the contracting agencies, and the Mayor's Committee on Human Resources, Inc., each had their particular interests to be satisfied, the main one being the employment of an individual loyal to their particular organization. The citizens were interested in a person they could work with and trust, one who was strongly committed to popular participation. The coordinating agencies, for their part, sought a person acceptable to the citizens but whose first loyalty would be to the agency, a person not so committed to popular participation that he would, for example, support the citizens in an attack on the agency. The MCHR, as the official city-wide agency responsible for both the coordination and the direct-service aspects of the antipoverty program, is in a somewhat tenuous position if and when conflict arises between these components; both would turn to the MCHR for support, using whatever forms of political pressures that are available—which would make life at the MCHR somewhat uncomfortable and could even jeopardize the entire program. Thus, the MCHR had an im-

71

plicit preference for a coordinator predisposed toward a cooperative, as opposed to a conflict-oriented, approach to his job, a preference that essentially coincided with that of the contracting agencies.

No formal credentials were required for the coordinator's position. Although the citizens gave some consideration to professional and educational qualifications, they viewed the applicants' prior experience, attitudes, and commitments as equally, if not more, important. The contracting agencies held varying attitudes concerning formal credentials. ACTION-Housing did not actively seek out professional social workers; the executive director of this agency expressed his preference for "hard-nosed" administrative types, a category that he considered eliminated most social workers. The four coordinators finally hired by this agency did not have social work degrees or backgrounds. In contrast, the four settlement houses, which had a professional status to maintain in the social work community, all hired coordinators with social work degrees.

In addition to loyalty, attitudes, and qualifications, two other factors were given significant attention in selecting the coordinators—race and residence. Although the coordinating agencies and the MCHR were reasonably attuned to these factors (because of the "political" nature of the job), it was primarily the citizens who pushed them to the forefront. There were two reasons for this emphasis. The first was based on a generalized citizen suspicion of "outsiders" and empathy for "one of their own kind." This set is illustrated in a citizen evaluation which—in recommending a neighborhood person for at least one spot on the coordination staff— stated that "it is very difficult to understand and to establish the rapport with the neighborhood that is needed without being a resident."[1] Implicit in all this seems to be the belief, of somewhat questionable validity, that those who have lived with a problem are in the best position to understand it.[2]

[1] South Oakland Citizen's Council, "Evaluation of Coordination," March 1967, p. 3 (mimeographed).

[2] In the process of adjusting to a harsh environment, what is defined as a problem by the American middle-class majority can become an acceptable part of life for the poor; sometimes, those who learn to live with a

The Professional Organizers

The second, more latent, reason for stressing racial and residential criteria was the desire to get some of the "gravy" for the folks—that is, jobs. Local people, especially Negroes, long deprived of significant opportunity and mobility, while at the same time acculturated to the idea of local patronage, saw a chance for these attainments in the coordination unit, particularly in the positions of assistant coordinator, which were more accessible to those without a college background. Generally, the citizens who were most active in the program were the ones involved in decisions concerning these job descriptions; they were also the ones most likely to be hired. Thus, in every neighborhood, a residence preference was stated in the job description. The racial preference, being too "sensitive" an issue and applicable primarily to the Negro poverty areas, was not formally expressed in the job description. However, the preference was in effect in the three antipoverty neighborhoods with large Negro populations—the Hill District, Homewood-Brushton, and Northside—all of which wanted and got Negro coordinators.[3]

The actual procedures used in selecting the neighborhood coordinators allowed for a balancing of interests between the citizens, the contracting agency, and the Mayor's Committee on Human Resources, Inc. Most candidates were recruited by the contracting agency, which allowed, initially, for an informal type of screening to occur, since the job opening was usually publicized

---

problem no longer see it as such, or see it at all. Planned change, which involves stimulating an awareness of difficulties, eradicating difficulties, and positive action to improve upon already favorable circumstances, requires the ability to perceive both what is and what might be. For example, see Ronald Lippitt, Jeanne Watson, and Bruce Westley. *The Dynamics of Planned Change* (New York: Harcourt, 1958), pp. 132, 159–161.

[3] When the North Side coordinator resigned, the citizens' council voted unanimously to have Richard Ridenour, a white man, moved into the position. Prior to this, Ridenour had worked in the neighborhood for almost a year as an assistant coordinator. In that time he had been put to the test; having participated in over one hundred citizens' meetings and marched on numerous picket lines, his commitment to working with and for the citizens was verified through action. However, it should be noted that the Northside is far from being a black ghetto (about 25 per cent Negro), and that race continues to be a significant issue in this and other neighborhoods.

only to a select audience. The candidates were then interviewed by a personal committee of residents, which made recommendations to the contracting agency. Basing their decision, in part, upon these recommendations, the agency selected an individual for the position and communicated the choice to the neighborhood board for approval. Without the citizens' approval, the coordinator could not be hired. If their approval was given, the candidate's name went to the MCHR for final acceptance. Although each of the three parties had formal veto power, it never had to be utilized, since informal communications and bargaining resolved disputes before they reached this point.

The role of the citizens' personnel committee was very delicate, particularly when a local resident was in the running for the coordinator's position. An incident that occurred in Lawrenceville is illustrative. Here, one of the candidates for the coordinator's job was an active member of the newly organized neighborhood council. This person conducted a miniature political campaign during the selection period. His participation at neighborhood meetings was aggressive and studied to portray a tough, practical, and dedicated citizen, one who staunchly defended the interests of his neighborhood; he also pursued his case behind the scenes, twisting lapels and otherwise bringing pressure to bear upon the members of the personnel committee. Some members were intimidated by these tactics, a few were impressed, and others just felt uncomfortable; on the whole, the committee was placed in an awkward situation. While the local applicant was busy developing a constituency in the neighborhood, the other candidates had little opportunity to present themselves beyond the formal interview. There would have been no contest for the position if one of the nonlocal candidates had not made an outstanding impression upon the committee; also, it was obvious that this candidate was well received by the contracting agency. (The agency's attempts to exert pressure upon the committee were apparently negligible.) Thus, the committee was faced with a situation in which the political implications of favoring an "outsider" had to be carefully weighed against the personal qualifications of the candidate and the contracting agency's implicit preference.

The Lawrenceville citizens' council was at that time in an embryonic stage, and striving to develop an independent image. This was one of the first major decisions for which the council would take responsibility, and a miscalculation could well bring the opprobrious criticism of "selling out," thereby shattering the image before it gained substance. The final decision did not come easily. There were a series of tense meetings during which the committee deliberated the various issues. In the end, the pressure to hire the neighborhood candidate was tempered by the committee's desire to fill the position with the man who they felt was most qualified to do the job; the candidate from outside the neighborhood was selected as the committee's first choice, and was subsequently hired.

The committee's choice was not without negative repercussions, but, in retrospect, it appears to have been a wise one. Shortly after this decision was made, the local candidate was instrumental in organizing a segment of the neighborhood to withdraw from the program. Ostensibly, this withdrawal was based upon the contention that the area under consideration, although it fell within the geographic limits of Lawrenceville, did not meet the "poverty criteria" and that its residents did not need or want outside assistance. However, the whole affair had a strong undercurrent of racial prejudice; citizen fears were aroused; rumors spread that designation as part of a Community Action Program target area was part of a surreptitious plot for racial integration. This struggle for withdrawal constituted the most vicious and dirty episode in the brief history of Pittsburgh's antipoverty movement. Ironically, the battle was fought not by the underprivileged against some establishment enemy, but between potential allies.

Only a few of the experiences in hiring the coordinators were as involved as that of Lawrenceville, and few adhered so rigorously to the formal selection procedures. The selection procedures were most flagrantly abandoned in East Liberty-Garfield, where the first coordinator was selected by the director of the contracting agency, and citizen participation merely entailed the ratification of his choice. The candidate was matter of factly presented to the neighborhood board as the coordinator, with a request that they forward a letter of approval to the MCHR. The citizens quietly complied; no interviews were held by a personnel committee, and no alternative candidates were suggested. This experience occurred, in part, because the program was new and the ground rules were not firmly established. The director, acting in good faith, was anxious to get the program moving. He followed the traditional settlement-house mode of operation, which did not involve giving citizens serious responsibility for the selection of staff. Although informed of their right to contest the director's choice and play a more significant role in the selection process, the citizens accepted the situation. A change in power relationships is difficult for citizens to cope with, particularly when the traditional authority continues to take the initiative and assert itself, rather than emphasizing a new, more responsible role for the citizenry.

STRUCTURAL RESTRAINTS

The selection process illustrates how the coordinator is responsible to three groups, with overlapping but not coincident interests. This is a structural arrangement that operates to divide loyalties, confuse roles, and inhibit functioning. In evaluating the coordination structure, the citizens of at least one neighborhood explicitly noted that it creates an "inoperative relationship," one in which the coordinator "is torn among the wishes of the citizens' council, the financial control of the funding [contracting] agency, and the policies of the Mayor's Committee on Human Resources."[4]

If not totally inoperative, the structure is certainly unwieldy, anchored more in the principle of control than of action. Each of the three groups employing the coordinator wants to know, in terms of its own needs, what was accomplished yesterday, what is being worked on today, and what is planned for tomorrow. These demands are realized in the form of reports, phone calls, meetings,

[4] South Oakland Citizen's Council, "An Evaluation of Neighborhood Coordination," March 1967, p. 2 (mimeographed).

and a sea of paperwork; the coordinator spends an inordinate amount of time just trying to stay afloat. Multiple accounting of this sort sacrifices time, energy, and productivity to control, and, as a by-product, inhibits flexibility and action. This common bureaucratic phenomenon is here intensified by the presence of three sets of organizational interests and by the volatile political nature of the job.[5] To escape or minimize the pressures to satisfy a diversity of interests, the coordinator must often act on the principle of least friction, or he must maneuver furtively. Sometimes, through selective response to one or another of these pressures, the coordinator is able to guide his own course of action; but this involves the willingness, and—more important—the ability, to play politics.

Political considerations enter in as seemingly simple a task as designating the outdoor sign for the office. Should it be identified with the citizens' council, the contracting agency, or the MCHR? If all three, in what order should they appear? Who should get the biggest letters? Issues like this, which have little effect upon the core of the program, nip away with vexation at its husk.

More significant and complex problems exist, particularly the ones generated by the role of the coordinating agencies within the overall antipoverty structure. These agencies not only employ the coordinating staff, but they also contract with the MCHR to provide direct services in program areas like housing, employment, and family life. In the North Side, for example, the employment, family service, and coordination units all are contracted to Neighborhood Centers Association, a local settlement house. The North Side coordinator, as he aids citizens in their evaluatory review of proposed or actual programs in these areas, is thereby faced with a distinct and serious conflict of interests. The citizens are entitled to his services and honesty, his integrity and professionalism call for objectivity, while his job security, economic welfare, and bureaucratic status are controlled by a settlement house that is certainly

[5] For example, see Robert K. Merton, *Social Theory and Social Structure* (Glencoe, Ill.: Free Press, 1964), pp. 197–202; and Peter M. Blau, *Bureaucracy in Modern Society* (New York: Random House, 1963), pp. 105–110.

not anxious to have criticism directed at any of its operations.

In some areas, such as the North Side, East Liberty-Garfield, and the Hill, the contracting agency also employs neighborhood development units that are funded outside the antipoverty structure (through the Community Chest or other sources). The philosophy and responsibilities of neighborhood development and coordination staffs are very similar, any difference being more of degree than of kind. Generally, the neighborhood development worker provides service to smaller or sectional groups within the larger target area, and the coordinator focuses upon community-wide organizations. However, there are many exceptions to this arrangement, with both staffs often working simultaneously on both levels. Although the stated goal is to maintain a cooperative and reinforcing relationship between these units, neither is functionally dependent upon the other for fulfillment of its specific tasks.[6] Instead, both often compete for the time, energy, and confidence of citizen leaders, and both seek special recognition for the roles they play in whatever local victories are achieved. Such a structure places the contracting agency in a particularly strategic position to control both staffs, and, through them, the citizenry; for example, by physically separating these units in different facilities, regulating the flow of information between them, and judiciously utilizing incentives and sanctions, the agency, if so inclined, could discourage the development and consolidation of power in one community-wide citizens' group.

Although the formal structure does not facilitate clearly defined bureaucratic relationships, interdependence, and cooperation, it is possible that a harmonious relationship between coordination and neighborhood development staffs could be established informally. To a large extent, the success of such a structure would depend upon personal variables such as age, experience, and attitudes; the staffs could transcend the formal structure and collabo-

---

[6] The implications of "functional autonomy" for intraorganizational conflict are discussed by Alvin W. Gouldner in "Organizational Analysis," *Sociology Today,* ed. Robert K. Merton, Leonard Broom, and Leonard S. Cottrell, Jr. (New York: Harper, 1965), pp. 419–423.

rate in a fruitful effort if these variables were complementary. For instance, this result could be expected if either the coordinator or the neighborhood development worker were clearly the "top man" by virtue of status characteristics, skill, and personality, and the other were clearly the junior partner. Informal hierarchy would fill the void of formal hierarchy. However, in reality, the nature of these positions is such that they demand similar individuals.

Thus, the coordination structure in almost half of Pittsburgh's target neighborhoods provides fertile ground for internal conflict. The fact that internal conflict has been confined to seemingly minor skirmishes rather than being expressed in all-out warfare testifies not to any logic of structure, but to the ingenuity of the professionals involved and their ability to operate under strain.

RUNNING THE ENTERPRISE

In addition to organizing citizens and helping them to plan and evaluate neighborhood services, the coordinator is responsible for assuring that these component services are effectively working together in a comprehensive effort to eradicate poverty. Ideally, this means that the units must be willing to pool their skills, knowledge, manpower, and resources in a cooperative venture. To illustrate, take the hypothetical case of a welfare client entering the neighborhood service center to report to the receptionist that the ceiling in her apartment has collapsed, damaging some of the furniture. What should follow is something like this: the case is referred to a family service worker, who gets all the details from the client; the neighborhood lawyer is asked by the family service worker to find out if the landlord is responsible for making repairs and paying the cost of damages; in the course of his investigation, the lawyer learns that the landlord owns a number of slum dwellings in the neighborhood; he reports this to the coordinator, who, in turn, calls a meeting with the citizens' housing committee to discuss the problem; the committee decides to approach the landlord, requesting that he upgrade his properties, but he refuses; the health aides are sent out to inspect the properties, the lawyer is asked to review the ramifications of a rent strike, and the citizens form a picket line

79

around the landlord's home in suburbia. While the landlord is taking an impromptu vacation in Florida, the family service worker has not forgotten the client; the public-assistance consultant is asked to obtain a relocation grant, the employment worker is called upon to place the client in a work-training program, the client's children are enrolled in the local day-care center, and other local resources, such as homemakers and planned parenthood, are also utilized in an exhaustive effort to move the client out of poverty.

This example suggests how the component services might be integrated in a comprehensive attack on poverty—an ideal rarely achieved. In the actual situation, it would be discovered that the lawyer could provide service to the individual client and thereby advise on the landlord's responsibility for damages. However, he could not counsel the citizens' committee on the legality of a rent strike, since providing service to a group is against agency policy; the rationale is that, by pooling resources, the group could afford to buy this service in a private market. The health aides would need organizational permission to leave the area that they were currently inspecting in order to focus an intense effort upon the landlord's properties, dispersed throughout the neighborhood; their moving would conflict with the Allegheny County Health Department's service strategy, which involves saturating the neighborhood with inspections section-by-section. The Planned Parenthood unit could provide immediate birth control assistance only if the client was graced by holy matrimony; otherwise, this agency's policy dictates that certain procedures, such as obtaining parental consent for girls under 21 or somehow establishing that they are "clearly emancipated," first be fulfilled. Although the public assistance consultant could check on the availability of a relocation grant, like the others he has no power to transcend the rules and regulations of his agency, and grants of this nature are generally not provided by the Allegheny County Department of Public Assistance.

Each service unit is thus part of an autonomous organization with its own goals, policies, and needs—which are at times different than those of the coordinator, the client, and the citizens. These service units work together in the sense of being situated, usually,

80

The Professional Organizers

under one roof in one neighborhood service center. Although this proximity facilitates communications, it does not dictate cooperation. The neighborhood service center is structured to operate not along the lines of traditional bureaucratic organization, but as an "enterprise"—an impermanent and loose association of relatively autonomous organizations seeking to achieve common goals.[7] Four important features of the enterprise are: (a) *Complexity*—The neighborhood-center enterprise represents a mixture of public, private, civic, and religious organizations. Some are neighborhood-based, others have city, county, or nation-wide affiliations. The sheer number of participants is enough to complicate administration. (b) *Authority*—The participants are not bound to a formal hierarchy of positions based upon the element of rational-legal authority. Thus, informal relationships are more significant and behavior less predictable than in a traditional bureaucracy. For example, in one neighborhood, the director of a family service unit even refused to allow the coordination staff (who were professional social workers like herself) access to case files because of personal incompatibility. (c) *Reciprocity*—The lack of formal hierarchy means that some element other than rational-legal authority is needed to coordinate membership activities. In the enterprise, this element is reciprocity; members respond to one another more on the basis of mutual benefit than of individual advantage. This type of relationship may be established if members have similar norms and conceptions of reality and if a degree of solidarity exists within the organization.[8] (d) *Fluidity*—Organizational participation in the enterprise may expand and constrict because of spontaneous or

---

[7] For an analysis of the "enterprise" concept as it applies to urban renewal, see George S. Duggar, "The Relation of Local Government Structure to Urban Renewal," and Jewel Bellush and Murray Hausknecht, "Entrepreneurs and Urban Renewal: The New Men of Power," in *Urban Renewal: People Politics and Planning,* ed. Jewel Bellush and Murray Hausknecht (New York: Anchor Books, 1967), pp. 179–188, 209–223. This concept is also discussed by Scott Greer in *Urban Renewal and American Cities* (New York: Bobbs-Merrill, 1967), p. 36.

[8] Coordination through reciprocity as an alternative to a bureaucratic hierarchy is discussed by Robert A. Dahl and Charles E. Lindblom in *Politics, Economics, and Welfare* (New York: Harper, 1953), pp. 237–238.

prearranged action. Such shifting of participation may reflect an agreed-upon plan (as with the Summer Headstart program) or an arbitrary unilateral decision (as when the Bureau of Employment Security, without notice, reduced its staff commitment to the neighborhood employment units).

As one participant among many in the neighborhood-center enterprise, the coordinator does not possess coercive power and has only very indirect, if any, access to remunerative power. Thus, compliance with his administrative directives is not very much influenced by the threat of punishment or by the incentive of financial gain. Instead, it is the "ideal motives of solidarity" (Weber) or the "inculcation of motives" (Barnard) upon which the authority structure rests.[9] Essentially, this involves the use of normative power —the allocation and manipulation of symbolic rewards and deprivations—to produce acceptance or rejection, encouragement or embarrassment.[10]

Socialization is an important mechanism for ensuring the effectiveness of normative power. Through this process, organizational norms are internalized and commitments to goals are developed.[11] At the beginning of the Pittsburgh program, training and orientation sessions were held for the professional and nonprofessional staff of most agencies participating in the enterprise. These sessions ostensibly focused upon the etiology of poverty and the

[9] Max Weber, *The Theory of Social and Economic Organization,* ed. Talcott Parsons (New York: Free Press, 1947), p. 325; Chester Barnard, *The Functions of the Executive* (Cambridge: Harvard University Press, 1938), pp. 149–153. Also see Terence Hopkins, "Bureaucratic Authority: The Convergence of Weber and Barnard," *Sociological Theory,* ed. Lewis Coser and Bernard Rosenberg (New York: Macmillan, 1957), pp. 159–171.

[10] Amitai Etzioni suggests that there are two kinds of normative power: pure normative power and social power. The latter is more common in horizontal relations and is based upon the allocation of acceptance and positive response as opposed to esteem and prestige. See Etzioni, *A Comparative Analysis of Complex Organizations* (New York: Free Press, 1964), pp. 4–6.

[11] Etzioni, pp. 40–44.

community-action strategy for attacking this social disease. Most significant here was not learning the facts of poverty, but developing an "esprit de corps" and a broad identification with the antipoverty movement; the necessity of transcending agency goals and building staff commitments to the goals of the enterprise was continually stressed. This indoctrination also helped to confirm the legitimacy of the coordinator's authority, by weaving it into the fabric of the program's philosophy and goals.

Although these sessions undoubtedly had some impact, it would be an exaggeration to suggest that, in terms of establishing the coordinator's authority, they did more than set the stage. The coordinator's ability to elicit cooperation was actually determined through the interaction of personalities when the community-action drama unfolded in the neighborhoods. In the traditional bureaucracy, the lines are already written and the play is performed more or less in the spirit of formalistic impersonality—" 'Sine ira et studio' without hatred or passion, and hence without affection or enthusiasm. The dominant norms are concepts of straightforward duty without regard to personal consideration."[12] In contrast, the enterprise is less of a play and more of a "happening"; the actors move on and off stage at will, and the expression of individual personality is central to the performance.

A comparison of the Neighborhood Legal Service Association staff in two neighborhoods clearly exemplifies the relevance of the personality factor in running the enterprise. In the North Side, the attorney for the legal service component was an integral part of the community action team; he worked in close cooperation with the coordinator, attended staff meetings regularly, aided citizens' committees, and, when necessary, exhibited extraordinary flexibility and commitment by providing services outside the official range of his agency. On at least one occasion he aroused the displeasure of his boss, the Director of the Neighborhood Legal Service Association, by providing counsel on an issue concerning the reform of the minor judiciary. Although the director candidly expressed sympathy with this cause, it was a politically sensitive issue, and he did not

[12] Weber, p. 340.

want to have his agency identified as a protagonist. The North Side attorney's attitude is very well expressed in the words of those he serves in the neighborhood:

> Mr. Stefanko has functioned remarkably well as an advocate of the poor. We are constantly impressed by his insight and feelings for those who are disadvantaged through no fault of their own.
>
> He has helped with advice on how to proceed with changes and what pitfalls to avoid. He has been a speaker on many occasions to various citizens' groups and PTA's and has stood his ground well with his fellow lawyers.
>
> We want to acknowledge the evident sincerity, dedication, and competency of Mr. Stefanko and approve of his professional contribution to the clients he serves, the committee he aids, and the community at large. We appreciate his competence as well as his deep humane concern and commitment to his role as advocate of the poor.[13]

In contrast to these words is a memorandum from the chairman of the citizens' welfare committee in South-West—asking for their attorney's resignation. In no uncertain terms it states: "We don't want the present attorney because of his attitude toward the poor."[14]

In his refusal to accept the recommendation, the Director of the Neighborhood Legal Service Association pointed out that the charges against this lawyer had little to do with his professional competence. Rather, he was criticized for not having the very same personal qualities for which the North Side attorney was praised: an attitude of concern towards the poor, a willingness to cooperate with the enterprise, and a flexible approach toward service. His lack of cooperation was reflected in continued absence from interagency staff meetings, and in broken appointments with coordination staff; his rigid approach to service was illustrated by his refusal to follow up on the relatively few clients referred out of his office to another

[13] North Side Committee on Human Resources, "Evaluation of Legal Services of the North Side," April 5, 1967, p. 5 (mimeographed).

[14] Memorandum from the chairman of the South-West Welfare Committee, subject: Recommendations for Neighborhood Legal Service Association, May 2, 1967.

service; his negative attitude toward the poor was less clearly documented, but very strongly felt—in fact, he was nearly picketed.

The coordinators in the North Side and South-West were both professional social workers, aggressive but affable, and without any apparent personality disorders. Their attempts to integrate the legal aid component into the neighborhood-center enterprise were, to begin with, hindered by their lack of formal authority and complicated by the status differential that exists between social work and law. The attorneys were both formally qualified professionals working under the rules and regulations of the same legal service agency. Thus, in each situation, there were two professionals working within the same types of structures under similar constraints. Only the personalities of those involved account for the relatively easy integration in one setting and the almost completely independent legal operation in the other.

However, few staff members participate with the vigor of the North Side attorney, and few are as reluctant to cooperate as the South-West attorney. Most of the component agency staff fall somewhere between these two extremes. The coordinator is able to exert his authority upon those at the cooperative end of this continuum through the use of normative power. At the other end of the continuum are those who respond very erratically, if at all, to this form of authority; these are usually staff from the more powerful and more established of the participating agencies, such as the Bureau of Employment Security, the Board of Public Education, and the Allegheny County Health Department. The rigid bureaucratic mode of operation characteristic of these agencies extends right out to their antipoverty staff in the neighborhood centers. More than in the case of other members of the enterprise, the actions of these personnel are circumscribed by the firm rules and regulations of their agencies. Worth noting is the outstanding and somewhat unanticipated exception to the sluggish cooperation of the larger component agencies—the Catholic Diocese, whose staff was remarkably flexible and dynamic. This exception may be explained in part by the quest for relevancy, among religious organizations, through involvement in secular movements.

Clients or Constituents

In situations in which normative power is not sufficient to elicit compliance, the coordinator may, through a complicated and very indirect process, attempt to exercise remunerative power over personnel and agencies. This process is accomplished by means of the formal periodic citizen evaluation of programs, agencies, and personnel. In these evaluations, the citizens rely heavily upon the coordinator for information, advice, and technical assistance. Thus, more than any other staff person in the neighborhood, the coordinator is able to influence the recommendations that emerge from these investigations, recommendations that may advise expanding, limiting, or eliminating a component service. Frequently, after investigating a program and conferring with the coordinator, citizens delegate to him the task of writing up the evaluation. Sometimes when they are extraordinarily busy, tired, or apathetic, they leave to him the total responsibility for the entire investigation and evaluation. In either case, the evaluation must have the final approval and support of the citizens before it is sent to the MCHR.

The attempt to exercise this type of power encounters many difficulties. First, practically speaking, for this power to be viable, those who are expected to respond must perceive a cause-effect relationship between their behavior and any consequences. Since evaluation and refunding is a months-long process, the reaction, if any, is a delayed one. In terms of reinforcing authority, this procedure is far less potent than the swift allocation of sanctions and rewards —the bonus or the "pink slip"—employed by most organizations operating on the principle of remuneration. Also practically speaking, the actual impact and consequences of these evaluations are, at best, minor; that this secret is not very well kept certainly does not add to the coordinator's authority, and may even detract from it.

Another problem relates to the simultaneous utilization of a dual compliance structure—normative and remunerative—in the neighborhood-center enterprise. The exercise of remunerative power is necessarily based upon an alliance between the coordinator and a specific party to the enterprise, the citizens; here the coordinator is functioning as a citizen advocate. The coordinator's right to exercise normative power, on the other hand, rests on an alliance of professionals dedicated to the abstract enterprise—with the coordinator functioning as a middleman. Once the Coordinator behaves publicly as an advocate and uses this role to exercise remunerative power, he ceases to be viewed as an essentially neutral middleman; thus, his capacity to utilize normative power is subsequently reduced.

ROLES AND LOYALTIES

Given the restraints, ambiguities, and conflicts in the coordinator's role, how does this professional perform? Is he an advocate or is he a middleman? Does he manage a delicate balance between these two positions? Some insights into the actual performance of the coordinator may be gleaned from the perceptions of those with whom he works. In terms of the coordinator's role, the data in Table 2 reveal that the staff of service agencies participating in the neighborhood-center enterprise describe him as a predominantly neutral agent, one who is equally helpful to citizens and agencies. Staff perceptions are much less consistent on the question of loyalty; here they are almost evenly divided between those who describe the coordinator's first loyalty as being to citizens and those who see it as being to agencies. The general picture of the coordinator that emerges from a staff perspective resembles more closely that of a middleman than of an advocate. The citizens, on the other hand, are more likely to see the coordinator as their advocate; although more than half the citizens view the coordinator as helping both groups, proportionately almost twice as many citizens as staff see his primary role as helping citizens, and two-thirds of the citizens see themselves as the object of his first loyalty. This suggests that the coordinators have mastered the essential political and social tools for operating under conflicting pressures in the public spotlight—mainly, the ability to present different faces to different people and interest groups.

Most of Pittsburgh's coordinators view themselves as advocates, and are personally committed to increasing the power and influence of neighborhood citizens; but their performance, with few exceptions, rarely measures up to full advocate status. An advocate

87

Clients or Constituents

Table 2

CITIZEN AND STAFF PERCEPTIONS OF COORDINATOR'S ROLE
AND LOYALTY[a]

	Percentage of Citizens	Percentage of Staff
Coordinator's Role:		
Primarily helps welfare agencies develop services for the neighborhood	4.7	3.8
Primarily helps citizens plan services for the neighborhood	28.1	15.4
Equally helps both citizens and welfare agencies to develop services	57.4	73.1
Helps neither of the above to develop services	5.5	7.7
No answer	4.3	—
Total	100	100
	(N=256)	(N=26)
First Loyalty of Coordinator:		
To MCHR or contracting agencies	27.3	38.5
To citizens	66.4	42.3
To none of the above	2.0	3.8
No answer	4.3	15.4
Total	100	100
	(N=256)	(N=26)

[a] The data on citizen board members and staff presented here and in subsequent tables come from a survey conducted in the spring of 1967. For further details see the Appendix.

must be single-minded, almost fanatical, in the dedication of his time, energy, and sympathy. The selection process, the delegate-agency-coordination structure, and the neighborhood-center enterprise—each, in its own way, militates against the enactment of this role; there are too many tasks to be accomplished and too many interests to be pacified. For example, in the summer of 1967, the

The Professional Organizers

North Side coordinator organized a neighborhood-wide program to upgrade slum housing—mainly through rent strikes. He was reprimanded by the MCHR and Neighborhood Centers Association (the coordinating agency), not because this activity was especially threatening to these organizations, but because it left him little time for other responsibilities relevant to the neighborhood-center enterprise. In this case advocacy did not involve a direct confrontation with agencies operating in the antipoverty structure. Nevertheless, the enactment of this role still posed real problems.

Thus, in answer to the question raised earlier, most coordinators respond to both agency and citizen interests, and in doing so walk the tightrope between advocate and middleman. To maintain this balance, they become masters at negotiation, accommodation, and manipulation of citizens and agency staff. This role is not one conducive to democratization and reform of social welfare.

CHAPTER V

Mechanism of Social Change

I n line with the major reform objective of the antipoverty movement, two mechanisms—citizen planning and citizen evaluation—were built into the Pittsburgh program to facilitate change in the decision-making structure and the operation of the city's welfare-related institutions. This change was specifically aimed in the direction of greater participation by citizens in the decisions concerning the service programs that would be established in their neighborhoods. The idea was to provide the citizens of poverty neighborhoods a formal opportunity to influence the persons and the programs supposedly serving them, an opportunity long denied the poor and more commonly available to middle-class consumers of education, health, and other welfare-related services.

The leverage for instituting this change was to be supplied, primarily, by the same incentive through which more affluent members of the society are able to influence such services—namely, money; here, however, it would be money supplied by the federal government. Simply stated, the strategy was that suppliers of service could expand their programs with federal funds only if the consumers of these services were involved in their planning and in the monitoring of their production. Theoretically, the planning aspect could work two ways, with either the citizens' councils or the agencies initiating a particular proposal for a neighborhood service program. If initiated by an agency, the proposal had to be submitted in detail for review by the neighborhood citizens' council before the MCHR would consider it for funding. If a proposal were initiated by the citizens and it entailed the utilization of available agency resources, an appropriate agreement would have to be reached with that agency before the MCHR would consider it. In either case, the final decision as to whether a proposal would be recommended to the Office of Economic Opportunity for funding rested with the MCHR Board. As this board contained neighborhood representatives, it was reasonable to assume that, if the mechanism functioned as theoretically planned, citizen influence would be maintained throughout the process.

However, in practice, the planning mechanism did not work out this way. In 1965, at the start of the program, almost all of the proposals were initiated by the agencies. From the very beginning there was an overload, and the planning mechanism jammed. The citizens were engulfed in a sea of agency proposals with little time

91

for explanation, discussion, and thought to determine their merits. Often the proposals were received by the citizens only a day or two before a decision was due, and sometimes the citizens' councils were bypassed altogether.

Thus, the planning process envisioned by the MCHR as a mechanism for change never really had a chance to develop and mature. In 1965 the citizens went through the motions of democratic procedure, but few were deceived; for the time, most citizens accepted simply exercising their rubber-stamp approval of proposals. The acceptance, by citizens and professionals, of this aborted process was partly due to the acknowledged need for the services thus provided. Even more important was a "something is better than nothing" psychology that prevailed during this period of rapid expansion. The seemingly bottomless well of federal resources had an intoxicating effect. Quantity rather than quality of service was emphasized; for if, as the thinking went, the resources were limitless, then why not absorb as many as possible now and worry about careful planning later?

However, later came all too soon when, the following year, the well of federal resources went abruptly dry, due to the parsimonious attitude of Congress toward the antipoverty program. No new funds were available for expansion, and programs all over the country were cut back on short notice. This signaled a rush for consolidation and, once again, the citizens were caught in a squeeze. This time the pressures came from a different direction; the rationale for hasty action, which in translation meant effectively by-passing the citizens, went from "getting as much as possible" to "saving as much as possible." The general attitude in Pittsburgh was that, unless the program were rapidly trimmed in line with the recommendations sent from Washington, the final cutbacks would be more severe. This attitude had some validity in light of the fact that the city was receiving a larger share of federal funds than was originally allocated for Pittsburgh by the Office of Economic Opportunity.

As the federal purse strings were drawn tight, there was little opportunity to initiate new proposals, and, toward the middle of 1966, the emphasis shifted from citizen planning to citizen evaluations as the primary leverage for change. From the very beginning of the Pittsburgh program, few citizens or staff perceived the true significance of the evaluation mechanism as an instrument for change. Those who were overenthusiastic viewed the mechanism as a simple cannon with which to blast the walls of recalcitrant institutions; the more cynical considered it to have about as much blasting power as a pop-gun. What most people did not recognize was that this mechanism could be either a cannon or a pop-gun, depending upon how it was loaded, handled, and aimed. The reason for this narrow thinking was largely based on misperceptions of the MCHR policy concerning citizen evaluations. Written into all contracts with service agencies was a clause establishing the right of the officially recognized citizens' councils to monitor the programs serving their neighborhoods. However, beyond sanctioning a general process, this policy never clearly articulated the possible implications. Many citizens were left with the impression that, to accomplish change, all they had to do was evaluate the programs and submit these evaluations to the MCHR for action. There was thus a confusion between being given the right to influence policy through evaluations and being given the actual power requisite for fulfilling this right. Many people assumed that the MCHR would be an automatic advocate of the neighborhoods, whereas, in fact, it functioned essentially as a middleman, a point which it did little to clarify for a year and one-half.

Thus, evaluations were submitted and citizens patiently awaited actions that were never taken; as with citizen planning, citizen evaluation meant little more than going through the motions. This result did not reflect any deliberate effort to deny citizens a voice in decision-making. On the contrary, the MCHR operations staff were firmly committed to the principle of citizen evalulation. However, the staff was simply not large enough to get the evaluation mechanism functioning properly. In the neighborhoods the coordination units were understaffed and had too many functions; downtown there was no Director of Research and Evaluation until the spring of 1966; and for the first eighteen months only four people worked on the operations staff. The primary function of the operations staff was to build the program and keep it running; their record of program expansion and consolidation under intense pressure suggests that there was little time for a system of quality control.

By the autumn of 1966, the first blush of excitement and success was beginning to fade. The program was fairly well established, and citizens were becoming bored and somewhat disillusioned with the empty motions they were making in the decision-making process. The president of the Lawrenceville citizens' council, in a letter to Mayor Barr, expressed the prevalent citizen discontent and the emerging citizen pressure for change:

> We believe it is time we look at the model plan and find out if it is operating as it was designed to operate. We in the neighborhood have understood the necessity of crash programs and the need for central planning in order to implement the many pieces of the program and organize the structure to conduct the program. With a tone of constructive criticism and as a member of the team that is responsible for the success or failure of Pittsburgh's Economic Opportunity Program, we offer recommendations. We no longer see operational haste as a legitimate explanation for by-passing citizen planning and evaluation functions. Our citizens, on a voluntary basis, invested more than 2,000 hours of work in evaluating EOA programs that were in operation in Lawrenceville during 1965. We are firm in our knowledge that many recommendations made in these evaluations would increase the effectiveness of the Economic Opportunity Program in Lawrenceville. Before any agency was to receive money for a new proposal, they were to negotiate with the neighborhood on the basis of the evaluation so that improvements based on the experience of a year's work would not be lost. If the agency would not negotiate with the neighborhood voluntarily, then it was the responsibility of the Mayor's Committee [on Human Resources] to see that such negotiations took place. If an agency would not negotiate with the neighborhood, the result would be that the agency would not be funded for operation in that neighborhood. . . . Most agencies, including the Mayor's Committee on Human Resources, Inc., are guilty of by-passing the negotiations with the neighborhood. . . . The model program and

methods of operation that were made under your leadership, Mayor Barr, is, in our opinion, so good that we will fight for actual practice to become one with the model.[1]

These statements are indicative of the growing pressure to activate the evaluation mechanism. However, operational confusion, lack of staff, and the pressure of time were not the only impediments to be confronted.

FRAGMENTATION

In addition to the problems just described, planning and evaluation had to cope with a serious structural-political weakness: each neighborhood operated as a separate unit, and thereby was too weak to generate the power to move large agencies. The 1966 citizen evaluations of the Board of Education's school-community agent program are a good illustration of this weakness. The school-community agent's job was to act, in a broad sense, as a liaison between local schools (one to three) and the neighborhood. While this person was formally a Board of Education employee and directly responsible to local school principals, he was also a member of the neighborhood-center enterprise and thereby responsible to the neighborhood coordinator and the citizens' council, although their control was based more upon informal agreement than bureaucratic authority. The job description and the organizational context was the same for all eight neighborhoods. Yet, as was frequently the case with city-wide programs, the citizen evaluations from different neighborhoods varied considerably; some were favorable, some unfavorable, and others indifferent. The crucial variable accounting for these differences was, once again (as with the Legal Service)', individual attitudes—in this case, mainly the attitudes of the local school principals; where the principals were community-oriented and responsive to citizens, the evaluations were generally favorable.

Thus, as the evaluations stacked up, the MCHR was faced

[1] Letter from Frank LaMarca, president, Lawrenceville Economic Action Program, September 19, 1966.

with conflicting pressures. Dissatisfied neighborhoods wanted the program restructured to allow the coordinator more formal control over the school-community agent. The Board of Public Education wanted the program to continue in its original form, which facilitated the principal's authority and allowed for bureaucratic control over staff; they pointed to the favorable evaluations to back themselves up. The satisfied neighborhoods (those with community-oriented principals) were fearful of upsetting the status quo and remained more or less neutral.

In this type situation, three ingredients are necessary for optimum citizen pressure:[2] *Comparable Constituency*—To swing weight with agencies that operate on a city-wide, or other than neighborhood, basis, it is important that a "grass roots" organization represent a constituency whose scale is comparable to that of the agency's service population. This consideration is essentially political and applies to "grass roots" organizations because their source of power is most often directly associated with the number of people ostensibly represented. *Consolidation of Forces*—Most "grass roots" organizations cannot claim a constituency on a city-wide scale. Thus, in attempts to move large agencies, the support of other groups must be sought. To be most effective, this support needs to be organized in such a way that the total constituency presents a united front. *Will to Action*—Finally, to optimize pressure, it must be clearly understood that the organization is willing to go beyond

[2] Jane Jacobs suggests that, for self-government, the district is a more functional organizational unit than the neighborhood: "The chief function of a successful district is to mediate between the indispensable, but inherently politically powerless, street neighborhoods and the inherently powerful city as a whole. The ideal neighborhood of planning theory is useless for such a role. A district has to be big and powerful enough to fight city hall . . . a district lacking the power and the will to fight city hall—and to win—when its people feel deeply threatened, is unlikely to possess the power and will to contend with other problems." Jacobs, *The Life and Death of Great American Cities* (New York: Vintage Books, 1963), pp. 121–122. She goes on to note that, in a city like Pittsburgh, 30,000 people may be sufficient to form a district (pp. 130–131). However, only one-half of the eight antipoverty areas contain a population of this size.

96

mere rhetoric and engage, if necessary, in direct action to bring about change.

In 1966 these ingredients were not present in the attempt, through evaluations, to change the school-community agent program. The citizens' councils advocating change represented only four neighborhoods, whereas the program served eight neighborhoods and the agency itself operated on a city-wide basis; each of the four neighborhoods acted independently; and, beyond presenting the evaluations, there was little indication of a strong will to action—indeed, when the program was refunded virtually intact, there were few even verbal protests, and these were not very loud.

PAROCHIALISM

To understand the fragmentation of citizen forces, it is necessary to understand the psychology of parochialism and its development in the neighborhoods. Parochialism was molded in three ways: by the myth of uniqueness, by the distribution of power, and by the city-wide leadership vacuum.

Myth of Uniqueness. The seeds of this myth were intrinsic to the organizing methods of Pittsburgh's citizens' councils, and are generally found in most "grass roots" organizing efforts. The method was to focus upon neighborhood problems, providing at once an acceptable reference group around which to organize and immediate issues with which the group could identify. Emphasizing the uniqueness of a neighborhood and its problems intensifies reference group identification and morale, which gives people the feeling of being special in their misfortunes and their right to improvement. This feeling is only a short distance from the attitude often expressed by citizens and staff in the Pittsburgh program—that every neighborhood has different (or special) problems and must fight for itself. This idea has at least surface validity based upon the diversity of urban life; but when this diversity is exaggerated to the point where huge similarities, particularly socioeconomic characteristics, are discounted as a basis for joint action, mythology has set in.

97

Clients or Constituents

Thus, although the stressing of the uniqueness of neighborhoods is initially functional in organizing people, it can become quite dysfunctional with regard to significant social change. Once the neighborhood vision and sentiment have been developed, it is difficult to extend beyond local borders—a result that gravely affects the range of problems considered within the "legitimate" sphere of group action, the manner in which these problems are defined, and the strategies put forth for solving them. For example, the problem of inadequate police protection would probably be defined simply as too few patrolmen in the neighborhood. The fact that, as with most public services, numerous interests are competing for what are generally limited resources would not enter this definition. Therefore, such solutions as increasing the overall pool of resources or reallocating the existing resources on a different basis would not enter the discussion. Instead, the neighborhood would bring pressure to bear directly upon the Public Safety Department or whatever city agency would consider the problem. If the pressure were sufficient, they could force a reallocation of resources, and the problem would be momentarily solved, at the expense, however, of some other neighborhood, most frequently a poor one. Thus, "special" problems are created, solved, and created again in a never-ending cycle that is the affliction of most American cities, especially of the low-income neighborhoods. While this process is occurring, the more affluent sections of the city are usually able to generate enough pressure to maintain a tolerable level of public goods and services.

The uniqueness of Pittsburgh's poverty neighborhoods is a myth. Although neighborhood issues do exist and can be important, most of their "special" and vital problems—such as inadequate housing, poor health, insufficient education, no jobs, and impoverished people—have the same roots, and these roots extend far beyond the borders of any single neighborhood.

Distribution of Power. The poverty neighborhoods vary in size, priority, and organizational sophistication. Each of these elements is an ingredient of power insofar as it influences antipoverty program development and resource allocation. The larger neighborhoods have *people power*—they draw upon the power of mass con-

98

stituencies (from 50,000 to 60,000 residents); neighborhoods high on the antipoverty priority list have *poor power*, based on their socioeconomic deprivations; and neighborhoods with sophisticated citizens' councils have *political power*—leaders, cadres, and organization. Although numbers and priority provide potential supports for power, organizational experience and sophistication are the essential and catalytic elements that convert potentials to reality and allow the neighborhood to wield actual influence. Some neighborhoods are characterized by a strong combination of these attributes, and others rank low in all three areas. Giving organizational sophisticatiton double weight, Table 3 roughly depicts the power distribution of Pittsburgh's eight poverty neighborhoods—based on these three variables.

This distribution of power operates to reinforce the psychology of parochialism, particularly where the differentials are greatest, as, for example, between the Hill District and Lawrenceville. The most powerful neighborhoods are not anxious to consolidate forces with those on the bottom of the list because they see themselves gaining little in the bargain. Acting alone, the citizens' councills in the Hill, Homewood-Brushton, and North Side neighborhoods could generate relatively strong pressure in their own behalf without the encumbrance of first compromising and resolving the interneighborhood differences that invariably arise when attempts are made to cooperate on joint ventures. Another factor vitiating against the consolidation of neighborhood forces is the distribution of power within the neighborhood councils. Each council contains a limited number of high-status positions, lodged primarily in the executive committees; in addition, a handful of people obtained a relatively high neighborhood status through the informal system— generally civil rights activists or "new breed" church leaders with strong local followings.

If the neighborhoods were to consolidate, powerful interneighborhood units would develop and inevitably overshadow and push out much of the local leadership. These new units could absorb some local leaders, but there would not be enough room at the top for everybody. Thus, the small group of leaders in each council

Clients or Constituents

Table 3

ESTIMATES OF NEIGHBORHOOD POWER[a]

Neighborhood	Size	Priority	Organizational Sophistication	Power Index
				[strong:]
Hill District	3	1	6	10
Homewood-Brushton	4	4	2	10
North Side	1	2	8	11
				[moderate:]
Southwest	2	5	10	17
Hazelwood-Glenwood	7	8	4	19
East Liberty-Garfield	5	3	12	20
				[weak:]
Lawrenceville	6	7	15	28
South Oakland	8	6	15	29

[a] Size is based upon 1960 census data; priority is based upon the designation of the antipoverty Planning Committee (discussed in Chapter III). The ratings of organizational sophistication were based on the author's judgments considering each neighborhood's history of community organization over the last 5 years (1963–1968) with particular emphasis upon the agency auspices. Thus, Homewood-Brushton and Hazelwood-Glenwood were rated as 1 and 2, respectively, because of the tenure and quality of community organization there under ACTION-Housing; the Hill District was rated as number 3 (higher than the other three neighborhoods, where settlement houses are engaged in community organization) because, in addition to settlement-house activities, it had civil rights groups and experience with urban-renewal-stimulated citizen activity; the other settlement-house neighborhoods—North Side, Southwest, and East Liberty-Garfield—clustered around the 4, 5, and 6 positions; prior to the antipoverty program, neither Lawrenceville nor South Oakland had ongoing community-organization activities, and therefore they were given an average rating of 7½.

has a vested interest in maintaining the neighborhood as the ascend-
ant structural unit in the program.

City-wide Leadership Vacuum. In 1965, two city-wide citizens' organizations developed that were closely tied to, but independent of, the antipoverty structure. These groups, Citizens Against
Inadequate Resources (CAIR)' and Citizens Against Slum Housing
(CASH)', were initially organized and staffed on a voluntary basis
by a few of the more social-action-oriented neighborhood coordinators, and their membership consisted mainly of citizens from the
various poverty neighborhood councils. Although membership and
staffing overlapped, CAIR and CASH had varying relationships
with the several neighborhood councils, ranging from formal sponsorship to little or no contact. These groups focused upon broad
issues rather than neighborhood problems, and the citizens and
staff participating were not preoccupied with the defense of neighborhood interests. However, the professional leadership was of necessity erratic, as the coordinators still faced the formal responsibility of their neighborhood-based operations and had neither the
time nor the energy to participate consistently on two fronts. Eventually, the staffing of these groups was passed on to other individuals and agencies.

During this period, a few coordinators also made sporadic
attempts to consolidate neighborhood forces within the antipoverty
structure around program evaluations. These efforts also involved
additional time and energy, and suffered from a further restraint:
none of the coordinators possessed the formal authority requisite for
assuming responsibility for and control of an interneighborhood
unit.

These attempts at city-wide organization suggest that the
psychology of parochialism was an effect as much as a cause of
fragmentation. Many citizens and neighborhood staff understood
the value of a cooperative interneighborhood effort, and many actually tried to consolidate around specific issues. Thus, although
fragmentation was a product of centrifugal forces generated by the
myth of uniqueness and the distribution of power between both

neighborhoods and individuals, the absence of a centripetal counterforce—leadership—cannot be ignored; the absence of this counterforce created a vacuous atmosphere in which the psychology of parochialism flourished. Clearly, the MCHR was responsible for and capable of providing city-wide leadership and direction to the poverty areas. It possessed the authority, legitimacy, and funds to catalyze the consolidation of neighborhood forces. But, as previously noted, during the first two years of Pittsburgh's program, the MCHR's organizational energies were focused upon program development rather than on social action and city-wide leadership of a citizen movement.

MCHR BOARD

The citizen members of the MCHR Board also contributed to the city-wide leadership vacuum insofar as they failed to back up the planning and evaluation mechanisms, to initiate policies for consolidation, or to push the MCHR staff into a leadership role. When the MCHR Board of Directors was first set up, it consisted of eleven delegates-at-large representing a broad range of institutional interests that, for the sake of brevity, may be characterized as those of the establishment, and three delegates representing the Negro community. Sixteen months later, eight neighborhood delegates were added to the board; seven of them were Negro, six were women. For the most part, these individuals came from the upwardly mobile middle-class-oriented groups in their communities.[3] None of them seemed to approach their job with a radical philosophy of citizen participation or social reform; on the contrary, regarding certain issues such as nonprofessional staff salaries and the size of public assistance grants, the citizen representatives often were more conservative than the "establishment" members of the board.

Between June 1966 and June 1967, the citizen delegates averaged a 75 per cent attendance rate at board meetings as com-

[3] After appointment to the board, two of these individuals obtained employment as nonprofessionals in the antipoverty program. They were thus placed in the somewhat compromising position of being able to influence policy decisions affecting the agency that employed them.

pared to a 57 per cent attendance rate for the other delegates. However, this high attendance rate was not coupled with aggressive participation. On the whole, the citizens listened attentively, contributed views and anecdotal comments on poverty, and sometimes asked questions, but rarely did they initiate any proposals. Most issues were perceived by the citizens in terms of neighborhood benefits, which, of course, affected the roles they played; seldom did they act as a unified interest group for the poor. When minor disagreements arose at board meetings, these were more often between citizen delegates, defending their respective neighborhood interests, than between the representatives of the poor and the representatives of the establishment.

For an agency ostensibly committed to such principles as innovation and democracy, the MCHR had rather monotonous board meetings. Seldom was the atmosphere electrified with a clash of ideas, a spark of creativity, or a challenge to authority. A small incident that occurred at one meeting provided—as illustrated by the board's reaction—a stimulating contrast to the "business as usual" atmosphere. At this meeting, a group of over twenty citizens from the Hazelwood-Glenwood neighborhood council had come for a hearing before the board. Their chairman presented a challenging statement "rejecting entirely the decision to cut the diocesan program from the CAP program in Pittsburgh," and noting that "neither you [MCHR] nor the OEO can continue to tell us that you desire citizen participation; send us endless memorandums to that effect; and then utterly reject the decisions and recommendations that we make."[4] When the statement was finished, the members of the board spontaneously broke into applause. Being challenged in this direct manner was apparently a new and exciting experience, one which evoked not hostility, but appreciation. However, incident such as this were few, and the citizen board members generally played little part in instigating them.

From the very beginning, three major factors militated

[4] Presentation by Dorothy Bellas, Education Committee Chairman of the Hazelwood-Glenwood Glen Hazel Extension Council, to the Board of Directors of the MCHR, March 31, 1967.

against the citizens' playing a more vigorous role as board members. First, timing was poor. Entering the board chambers more than a year after the program was launched, they had to adjust not only to the new experience of operating on an equal footing with members of the establishment, but also to functioning within the normative procedural framework that these individuals had already developed. The new members were thus outsiders (in terms of social class) and latecomers (in terms of appointment), and the latter intensified the former. The establishment members did not approach the newcomers with discomforting attitudes such as noblesse oblige; but nevertheless, as most upwardly mobile middle-class-oriented individuals, the citizens were keenly aware of social barriers. The second impediment to more vigorous participation related to the citizens' status as representatives. Of their own volition, the citizens were cast into the role of neighborhood spokesmen while the other board members acted as delegates-at-large. Generally, the citizens approached the board as individuals primarily concerned with defending their local interests rather than the interests of the poor. Thus, there was little mutual support. Finally, and perhaps most important, the citizens were inadequately prepared to assume their positions on the board. Whereas most of the delegates-at-large came to the MCHR with years of experience on agency boards, the citizens had only their neighborhood experience plus about four hours of training and orientation by the MCHR staff before they assumed the responsibility of guiding a complex multimillion-dollar project. Although experience at the neighborhood level had made citizens quite knowledgeable about program content, more so than the other delegates, they were not familiar with either financial complexities or normative behavioral standards for agency board members. This knowledge they learned, after being seated on the board, by taking cues from the establishment representatives, who themselves had little time for deep questioning of the philosophy or the strategy of the antipoverty movement and tended to lean heavily upon staff for direction.

As a whole, the board did not provide particularly dynamic leadership for the program, and the staff made few demands that would elicit such leadership. This type of performance is not unusual, nor is it limited to welfare agency boards. In most organizations, board members are volunteers with numerous roles and commitments in the community and other concerns more pressing than those of the agency that they serve; and many executive staff are generally rather content with boards that regularly accept their recommendations and guidance without too much fuss. However, as an organization supposedly dedicated to facilitating citizen influence, the MCHR raised certain expectations about the role of its own board; while the board's performance conformed to the conventional model, it fell far short of expectation as both a model and a driving force for the antipoverty movement.

CONSOLIDATION OF FORCES

Toward the end of 1966, it became apparent to all parties that the evaluation mechanism was functioning more as an education and therapeutic process than as an instrument for social change. It was also recognized that certain restraints were built into the very structure of neighborhood coordination (discussed in Chapter IV). Dissatisfied with this cumbersome structure and with the failures of the evaluation mechanism, citizens, neighborhood staff, and the MCHR began to pose alternatives. One such alternative was to bring the coordination units into the central staff. An in-house document circulated among the MCHR staff outlined some advantages and potential disadvantages of this arrangement:

Advantages

It would result in greater control, coordination, and communication with neighborhood staff.

It would greatly simplify operations and the flow of communications, eliminating much waste of time and confusion caused by various layers of authority.

It would minimize conflicting loyalties.

It would eliminate actual and potential conflict between MCHR goals and agency goals.

It would make for less neighborhood parochialism by providing a center from which coordination could mass city-wide efforts.

It would provide the MCHR direct access to neighborhood citizens' councils and dampen its image as an "outside" agency.

Disadvantages

It might upset the delicate political balance between social agencies, possibly resulting in difficulty in maintaining the cooperation of service units.

It might create conflict with agencies who refuse to relinquish their neighborhood strongholds and who would continue to operate their own community-development units (particularly in the Hill District and ACTION-Housing neighborhoods).

It might result in a partial exodus of present coordinators.

It might encounter resistance from neighborhood councils viewing the change as a further encroachment upon their independence.

It might result in a loss of citizen morale (particularly in neighborhoods where the coordination agency is deeply entrenched).

The MCHR staff thus anticipated resistance especially by contracting agencies to any scheme eliminating them from the coordination structure and thus forcing them to cut staff and budget and lose power—and few, if any, agencies voluntarily surrender power. With the citizens' support there would be a possibility of overcoming this resistance. But it was unlikely that citizens would applaud an alternative that simply substituted the MCHR for the contracting agencies; the citizens were habitually suspicious of the contracting agencies and periodically paranoid about the MCHR.

A second alternative was posed, which involved bringing coordination into the central staff for a limited period of time, during which the eight neighborhood councils would form a federation. After incorporating to obtain formal status as a nonprofit organization, the federation would receive the coordination contracts for all eight neighborhoods, thereby putting citizens solidly in the driver's seat. Aside from the economy of scale and the consolidation of power, a particular advantage of this scheme was that it would testify to the MCHR's commitment to citizen participation, a commitment seriously questioned in the neighborhoods.

At an MCHR staff meeting in November of 1966, the federation idea was discussed with much enthusiasm. There was a general consensus among the staff that the main function of this structure was to provide the citizens with some muscle in the welfare decision-making arena. The hope was that, through consolidation, the citizens' interests would be represented in this arena on at least an equal footing with those of the service agencies and other parties. This meeting, almost two years after the program began operation, marked the first concrete decision by the MCHR to provide city-wide leadership to the citizens' councils. At the end of the meeting, one of the more action-oriented staff commented: "This is the best meeting we had in two years. We are finally beginning to discuss what we are all about, and that is democracy."

Subsequently, the federation plan was presented for discussion to the citizens' councils in a series of neighborhood meetings; in almost every case it was firmly rejected. Among the various reasons for local opposition to the federation structure, the fact that the plan emanated from the MCHR cannot be ignored. From the neighborhood perspective, this origin provided grounds for suspecting an insidious plot. Many citizens and neighborhood staff found it difficult to believe that the MCHR was truly interested in fostering independent citizen action, and interpreted the plan as an attempt by the mayor to gain greater control over the neighborhood councils. Thus, from the start, the plan was viewed with a jaundiced eye. An even stronger reason for opposition was the previously discussed psychology of parochialism. After almost two years of operation with a strong neighborhood orientation, local councils had no desire to sacrifice their autonomy, power, and status; and many had fallen under the spell of the myth of uniqueness. The data in Table 4 indicate that, of the neighborhood board members who viewed the problems in their community as somewhat or very different from those of the other antipoverty areas, nearly two-thirds were opposed to federation. Also opposing federation were 55 per cent of the citizens who responded that the problems in their

Clients or Constituents

Table 4

Citizen Board Member Views on Neighborhood Problems and Federation ($N=244$)

Nature of Community Problems	Opinion on Federation					
	For		Against		Total	
	%	(No.)	%	(No.)	%	(No.)
Very Different	45.8	(11)	54.2	(13)	100	(24)
Somewhat Different	34.7	(25)	65.3	(47)	100	(72)
More or Less the Same	44.9	(62)	55.1	(76)	100	(138)
Exactly the Same	70.0	(7)	30.0	(3)	100	(10)

community were more or less the same as those of the other areas; however, when asked to specify reasons for their opposition, almost one-half of this group noted that they opposed the plan because their problems were really different. The following are samples of the attitudes often expressed: "This action [federation] would be in direct violation of the objectives of a neighborhood organization and against a neighborhood's interests." "Areas tend to have different and specific problems. The people in those areas understand them best and can work better toward a solution." "Each community needs a strong force of its own."

However, citizens were neither completely blind to the advantages of federation nor totally averse to the idea of contracting directly for coordination. On the contrary, as an alternative to the federation plan proposed by the MCHR, all of the neighborhoods opted for the development of a confederation, and four neighborhoods explicitly called for the immediate funding of coordination units directly under their particular neighborhood citizens' councils. As interpreted by local staff and citizens, the confederation was a less structured and less formal alliance than the federation, and thereby less threatening to neighborhood autonomy; participation in the confederation was viewed as strictly voluntary, with each neighborhood free to lend or withdraw its support on any given issue. In a proposal to the MCHR, the board of directors of the

108

Mechanism of Social Change

Hazelwood-Glenwood citizens' council specified some purposes of a confederation: (a) to provide for a stronger and broader base of citizen involvement and community organization; (b) to strengthen individual neighborhood committees and neighborhood citizens' councils through support from other citizens' groups; (c) to provide a unified policy and leadership for citizens' groups on a city-wide basis when they share common concerns; (d) to establish independent neighborhood citizens' organizations that would be formally incorporated; (e) to provide citizens an opportunity to unite for social action against status quo institutions (social action would utilize all legal methods to promote social, political, and economic change as necessary).[5] In suggesting methods for moving towards confederation, the proposal specifically noted:

> After a neighborhood has completed an evaluation of a specific program, the chairmen or delegates of all neighborhood program committees will meet to share evaluations. Those areas of agreement should be submitted to the MCHR Board of Directors as one document. When there cannot be agreement, individual neighborhoods will submit their own evaluations. The enactment of city-wide and neighborhood evaluations should be mandatory upon the MCHR Board.[6]

In the middle of 1967, the movement towards confederation began, with representatives from each council meeting as a group with MCHR staff to discuss action on the citizen evaluations of city-wide programs. The idea of funding coordination directly to citizens' groups was also explored with two neighborhood councils that chose to press this issue. The MCHR hesitated to discuss this idea with the other, apparently disinterested, citizens' councils, as immediate independent citizen funding for coordination was viewed by the MCHR as unlikely and undesirable. One of the first attempts at confederated action is described in detail in the following chapter.

[5] Hazelwood-Glenwood Glen Hazel Extension Council, "Proposal for Citizen Participation," February 7, 1967, p. 3.
[6] "Proposal for Citizen Participation."

CHAPTER VI

Confederated Action

In April of 1967 efforts were launched
to realize a citizen confederation. During this month a meeting was
held between the MCHR staff and the neighborhood Education
Committee chairmen to discuss the citizen evaluations of education
programs funded by the MCHR and to prepare, if possible, a unified position and set of recommendations relative to the funding of
these programs in 1968. Prior to this, six of the eight Education
Committee chairmen had agreed that their primary recommenda-

tion would be to refund the Kindergarten Aide program, which was apparently to be cut in the coming year. At the meeting with the MCHR staff, this decision was reaffirmed; although two neighborhoods were not in full agreement, it was tacitly understood that they would not oppose the majority. A second recommendation coming out of this meeting concerned the School-Community Agent program. The citizens wanted the job description of the School-Community Agent altered to allow for the possible employment of nonprofessionals in this position, and they wanted certain bureaucratic structural changes to make the position more responsible to the neighborhood coordinator. With these changes, the program would be recommended as the second priority for refunding.

The first recommendation was based upon the judgment that the Kindergarten Aides (nonprofessionals) were important because they provided extra classroom support, thereby freeing the teacher for more individualized attention; this judgment rested upon the pre-Kindergarten experience that many low-income pupils received in Pittsburgh's Head Start program. The nonprofessional School-Community Agent was seen as facilitating communications between the local school and neighborhood people. With both of these recommendations, an important, if less explicitly emphasized motive, was the desire to create and maintain nonprofessional employment opportunities.

Another issue related to the participation of citizens in non-OEO educational programs, particularly compensatory-type programs, funded through the Ford Foundation and the Elementary and Secondary Educational Act of 1965. A suggestion was made at the meeting that the Education Committees might include in their recommendations program priorities that encompassed all phases of educational programming, rather than just OEO-funded programs. Thus, philosophically, the citizens were wrestling with the deeper meaning of maximum feasible participation: as consumers of education services, as citizens, and as taxpayers, should they be involved with only OEO-funded programs, or should they attempt to exert influence and demand a voice in determining the total range of education services available? The suggestion was favorably received and was brought up repeatedly during the meeting; however, it was not stressed in the final recommendations.

The citizens chose to maintain a very limited program focus, as opposed to a broader approach that would have meant tackling the sizeable job of reviewing and ranking a multitude of Board of Education programs. Moreover, empirically, they had little reason to believe that such a mammoth effort would meet with much success. Thus, a relatively small and feasible battle was to be waged, one focusing on two OEO education programs—Kindergarten Aides and School-Community Agents.

The initial meeting ended with a discussion of how the citizens might present their case to the Board of Education. The problem here, as one member put it, was that "every time we raise our ugly little heads and complain they give us a pacifier." Or, in an equally cynical vein, "it's so hard; those men are so learned in double-talk. They tell us that 'we were not aware of that problem but we will look into it.' How can they be so unaware of so much?" These citizens were describing the frustrations they had experienced in their dealings with a very smooth, dedicated, and well-oiled team of professionals. The staff of the Pittsburgh Board of Public Education was particularly adept in the political art of defending the decision-making autonomy of their organization. Hence, it was decided that another meeting was necessary solely to plan strategy. At this meeting an attempt would be made to simulate, through role-playing, the confrontation between the citizens and the Board of Education staff, with the MCHR staff playing the adversary.

REHEARSALS

The second meeting was held a week later. The purpose of the role-playing session was to sensitize the citizens to the intergroup and interpersonal dynamics of their meetings with the central staff team of the Board of Education. Members of the MCHR had observed this team in operation over the last two years and had developed a healthy respect for the way these professionals worked in unison when confronted by neighborhood groups.

The MCHR staff, playing the role of this team, used the

112

same tactics that the real team invariably employed when confronted by citizens. The major ones were: *Controlling the Framework of Interaction*—The meeting was chaired by a member of the MCHR staff playing the Superintendent of Schools, Sidney Marland. The agenda and the seating arrangement were also prepared by the MCHR staff. The citizens, thus arranged and directed, then had to listen to twenty minutes of welcome and opening remarks by the "Superintendent" before they had a chance to speak.

Emphasizing Positives—Much of the content of the "Superintendent's" opening remarks, as well as the comments of his "central staff," emphasized the innovations and the achievements of Pittsburgh's public school system, particularly the new compensatory-type programs initiated with antipoverty funds, foundation grants, and Elementary and Secondary Education Act money. Successes were largely attributed to the "fine cooperation and support received from the neighborhood citizens in our common efforts to provide an excellent education for all of Pittsburgh's children." Also stressed was the continuing need for such cooperation and support if everything was not to be lost.

Maintaining the Offensive—After the first twenty minutes, the theme of "success through support and cooperation" was established. The "Board of Education team" had taken the initiative, and proceeded to follow it up through the rest of the meeting. Although citizens were pressed to substantiate each of their recommendations, the "Board team," when thus pressed, deftly maneuvered and maintained their offensive. For example, when the citizens asked why the School-Community Agent could not be a nonprofessional, the comeback was, "What do you see as the prime function of this program? Do you think that a nonprofessional should be allowed access to confidential files?"

Cooling the Opposition—Whenever the discussion started to get less than friendly, the "chairman" called two members of the "team" into action; a few corny jokes and some personal anecdotal references to the "folks" present provided enough comic relief to cool the atmosphere. At one point, when the discussion got somewhat heated, a deft parody of this tactic was employed as a "team member," in an attempt to "cool" a citizen, shouted, "But, Mrs. A., I live in your neighborhood." The humor of this remark was not lost on the citizens; they recognized the obvious lampoonery of this gesture. In actual meetings with the Board team, certain of its members often attempted to establish rapport with the citizens by emphasizing their residence, upbringing, and experience in the poverty neighborhoods.[1]

Each of these tactics was part of an overall strategy of consensus formation. The "Board team" was attempting to define the situation for the citizens in such a way as to eliminate the possibility of direct conflict.[2] They managed to get a good start by establishing a few central assumptions, specifically: that the Board of Education program was a success; that the success was in part the result of citizen cooperation and support; and that the continuance of this fine relationship was desirable and essential. From these assumptions flowed the expectations as to what would constitute the normative forms of behavior at the meeting, such as exploring common goals, cooperation, and polite and friendly discourse. To discredit these expectations, for example, by unexpectedly shouting demands and threats, would entail the risk of personal embarrassment generally felt when one does not adhere to the normative standards of group behavior—a large risk when group support is uncertain and when the norms are set by those of a higher socioeconomic status.[3] Few

---

[1] One viewpoint of what happens when the Board team meets with citizens is presented in the following "Statement on Oliver Situation by Parents Committee," November 16, 1967, p. 3 (mimeographed): "At the meeting last night, Dr. Marland and his staff tried every trick in the book to get us off the track. Marland packed the meeting with about a dozen of his staff prepared as 'experts' to put us down. He threatened to walk out of the meeting. They tried to divide the group against itself. They tried to decoy the group into discussion of minor and irrelevant issues. They tried to have the group appoint another smaller study committee which could be more easily influenced by the 'experts.' We saw through these games and held to the issue."

[2] For an analysis of the way individuals and groups attempt to structure situations to influence others, see Erving Goffman, *The Presentation of Self in Everyday Life* (New York: Doubleday, 1959).

[3] S. E. Asch, "Effects of Group Pressure on the Modification and

of the citizens were willing to contravene the "Board's" expectations and thereby expose themselves to this type of embarrassment. The session ended with the vague promise by the "Board" that it would "take the citizens' recommendations into consideration."

After the role-playing session, the MCHR staff and the citizens analyzed what had taken place. The staff explained to the citizens how they had allowed the "Board team" to structure the situation and how they had accepted a set of behavioral norms that called for a rational discussion rather than a negotiation, the difference being that a negotiation implied the use of more than logic to defend citizen recommendations. Not once had the citizens expressed a will to action by implying that some form of political pressure might be used to support their position. It was pointed out that in terms of building a rational argument, the "Board team" was more articulate, more sophisticated, and more informed than the citizens, and, starting from a different value base, could easily defend the logic of its position against the citizens' recommendations for change. Thus, without at least the threat of conflict, there was little to deter the real Board team from imposing its will upon the citizens if so inclined. The role-playing session clearly indicated that the citizens were not yet prepared to meet with the Board of Education, and it was decided that another strategy session should be held the following week.

The third meeting opened with the news that OEO guidelines for education programs would not be stringently applied to Pittsburgh. Although the amount of funds would be reduced, the allocation of these funds would be locally decided; the programs that rated high with citizens were thereby eligible for refunding. With this in mind, the members again turned the discussion to the impending session with the Board of Education. As in previous meetings, the citizens got bogged down in irrelevant and long-winded discourse concerning the worth of the Kindergarten Aide program and the necessity for altering the School-Community Agent program. Little thought, time, and energy were given to preparing

Distortion of Judgments," *Group Dynamics*, ed. Dorwin Cartwright and Alvin Zander (Evanston, Ill.: Row, Peterson, 1953), pp. 189–200, a strategy of direct action to support these recommendations. Although the futility of basing their case upon sheer rhetoric had been emphasized at the role-playing session, the point was lost at this meeting—the citizens were preparing for rational discussion rather than negotiation with the Board of Education.

By the end of this third meeting, signs of citizen restlessness appeared. Instead of completing their plans that day, they decided to meet a few minutes prior to the session with the Board of Education, at which time they would also elect a group chairman. No mention was made of drawing up an agenda for the meeting and, by default, the job went to the MCHR staff.

CONFRONTATION

The meeting between the citizens and the Board of Education took place a few weeks later in the MCHR conference room, an ostensibly neutral territory. About forty-five minutes before it began, the citizens and members of the MCHR staff met to consolidate their plans. The Executive Director of the MCHR, who presided at this pre-meeting gathering, started by suggesting a seating arrangement that placed the representatives of the citizen education committees up front and the Board of Education staff "in the classroom." Since members of only six of the eight neighborhood committees had shown up for this meeting, he advised seating two more people at the front table so that it would appear as if all eight neighborhoods were represented. Some discussion ensued about the citizens' presentation, with everybody stressing the importance of a united front, particularly in reference to the two major recommendations that would be made. The Executive Director selected a chairman for the citizens' group, and the Board of Education staff, already waiting in the hallway, was invited to enter.

The citizen chairman opened the meeting with the inaccurate but strategically sound statement that all eight neighborhoods were represented by the group at the front table. He followed with a presentation of the citizens' recommendations, and, for the next two hours, the reasons for and against these recommendations were

116

bandied about. The citizens were united in their arguments for having the Kindergarten Aide program refunded. On this issue, the Board of Education staff's position was that, although they wanted very much to continue the program, it appeared that not enough money was available because of the cutback in funds. They pointed out that the Kindergarten Aide program was not one of the Board of Education's "mainstream" projects, and thus was low on the Board's priorities for refunding; the criteria by which "mainstream" projects were judged as more important than those outside the "mainstream" were not clarified.

After the citizens presented their recommendations for altering the School-Community Agent program, a Board of Education member asked if the problems with this program were manifest in all eight neighborhoods. At this point, the unity among citizens began to dissolve as representatives of two neighborhoods disclaimed any problems in their communities. This breach was immediately picked up by a Board staff member. He suggested that the problems that did exist were perhaps the fault of the Education Committees; continuing on the offense, he gave discomforting examples of attending neighborhood Education Committee meetings at which only two citizens showed up, and topped these remarks by noting that maybe these committees should be evaluated instead of the program. In response, a citizen pointed out that the neighborhoods in which the program was running smoothly had dynamic School-Community Agents and community-oriented principals who were able to transcend the structure; in the other neighborhoods, these staffs were not as aggressive or community-oriented. Thus, rather than depend upon the fluctuation of personalities, the citizens wanted the School-Community Agent's responsibilities and duties clearly specified so that, regardless of the principal's attitudes or who held the agent's position, the job would be done in accordance with citizen expectations.

During the meeting, the Executive Director of the MCHR made frequent comments, mainly to summarize the issues under discussion. However, he did not once advocate the citizens' point of view, and his staff remained completely silent, thereby conserving the organization's surface neutrality. The Board of Education staff enacted its standard performance, stressing cooperation and reasonable discussion. Although these individuals were undoubtedly sincere in their desire to cooperate with the citizens, they clearly viewed cooperation in terms of exchanging points of view rather than sharing in decision-making; and they defended to the hilt their agency's decision-making autonomy. One member, in a less than subtle performance, attempted to establish rapport and show how closely he was working with the citizens by prefacing his comments with a highly personalized greeting to all of the Education Committee representatives: "I see that Mr. A. from the South Side is here tonight," and so on. Another opened his remarks with the obvious statement, "First, it should be clear for the record that we are very happy you are so concerned about these programs."

The meeting ended with the understanding that the Board of Education staff would recommend (to its Board of Directors) the refunding of the Kindergarten Aide program. However, the implication was that the recommendation would not place this program above "mainsteam" projects, and that the possibility of finding outside funds to continue it was slight. In relation to the School-Community Agent, the Board staff agreed to rewrite the job description, taking into consideration the citizens' recommendations, and to have a staff member meet with citizens in the neighborhoods to iron out local problems.

ANALYSIS OF PROCESS

The series of meetings just described ended with two somewhat vague concessions by the Board of Education staff. Their agreement to recommend the refunding of the Kindergarten Aide program was phrased in a manner that presented at least an illusion of citizen victory. The studied ambiguity preserved the all-important consensus and peace. It was an adroit maneuver that satisfied both sides and ended the discussion on a note of harmony and cooperation; but it evaded the principal issue—that of establishing clear program priorities.

Confederated Action

Everybody was aware that Board of Education policy, although formally made in the name of the Directors of the Board, was the work and decision of the staff. Thus it would follow that if the staff recommend refunding of the Kindergarten Aides, the program would be continued. Or would it? The hitch lay in the content of this recommendation, which was elusively by-passed during the meeting. Would the staff recommend that Kindergarten Aides be refunded before "mainstream" projects? If not, what priority would they place on refunding this program? Would their recommendations be only a perfunctory ritual, calling for the continuance of the program if new funds could be found to support it? These questions were not raised because of an almost tacit understanding that the citizens would not be so crude as to push the issue any further once the Board of Education staff agreed in principle that the program should be refunded.

In the final analysis, the confederation resembled more a debating society defending the logic of its position than a unified pressure group negotiating in its own behalf. A number of reasons explain why the citizens were unable to effect more than an exchange of views ending with an "agreement in principle." Foremost was their inability to comprehend the manipulation of power in the context of democratic bargaining. They based their actions on the notion that the transition from recommendation to implementation would be voluntarily and automatically produced through the force of sheer logic. However, in a pluralistic society, where different and sometimes conflicting interests coexist, such a process rarely occurs. Certainly different interests were at stake when the confederation faced the Board of Education; for example, the citizens emphasized increased nonprofessional employment at the expense, if necessary, of professional positions, and greater neighborhood control over certain professional school personnel. Both of these recommendations were somewhat incompatible with the interests of the Board of Education as a professional organization and as a bureaucracy. Under these circumstances, it was unrealistic for the citizens to assume that the Board of Education would voluntarily abdicate its position. On the contrary, in a pluralistic system, the Board had every right and reason to defend its interests staunchly.

The citizens did not recognize that, in the arena of public decision-making, logic is a firm support but no substitute for power, particularly when divergent interests are at stake. Starting from different value premises, most interest groups can construct sophisticated arguments to support their positions. They may meet, listen, and exchange views with the opposition, but there is no reason for them to alter their position until it is perceived that the opposition is willing and able to invoke sanctions or bestow rewards for such action.

Although the Board of Education staff were undoubtedly aware that the confederation possessed at least the seeds of power, they surely did not perceive in the citizens either the will or the ability to realize this potential. The confederation was without leadership; the appointed chairman of the group frequently addressed himself to the specific complaints of his neighborhood rather than to the confederation's interests. The confederation lacked a strong sense of unity, as reflected in the case of their division over the School-Community Agent program, an ostensibly common area of concern, and in their incomplete representation (only six out of eight neighborhoods). The confederation lacked the will to action; their presentation did not contain even a hint that they would jointly flex their muscles to stir the water of public criticism. Overall, the image projected by the confederation was not one to make an opponent quake.

These shortcomings reflected the citizens' lack of sophistication about the uses of power in a bargaining context and their inability to transcend the parochialism that reduces all issues to a neighborhood denominator. But what about the staff? Where was the professional leadership and guidance that might have clarified misconceptions about the negotiation process and helped to organize a potent citizens' pressure group? Although the MCHR had assumed the central responsibility for bringing the eight Education Committees together, its leadership was erratic, reflecting the dilemma of an organization that is committed to institutional cooperation at the same time that it is encouraging a challenge to institutional jurisdiction. Community-organization experience suggests that, when provoked by citizens' groups, institutions frequently react against the sponsoring agency.[4] Thus, in sponsoring the confederation, the MCHR was placing its relationship with the Board of Education in jeopardy.

The MCHR leadership was impaired not only by this built-in pressure, but also by the fact that at various points in the organizing process, three individuals, each with his own conception of the MCHR's role and his own style of leadership, acted as staff to the citizens. The first meeting was staffed by the Director of Operations, who, while committed to citizen participation, was cautious about planning for direct action under MCHR sponsorship. His style of leadership was relatively nondirective, and the meeting was process-oriented; although the citizens' complaints and dissatisfactions were thoroughly aired, no coherent plan of action emerged. The next meeting was staffed by the Director of Research, who was less concerned than the Director of Operations about protecting the MCHR's relationship with the Board of Education. His approach was more radical and directive, advocating that the citizens prepare to bring strong pressure to support their interests; he presented a number of action alternatives. However, the staff became so involved in the advocate role that the citizens got little opportunity to participate and internalize the message. Again no consensus was achieved on a specific course of action. The third meeting, called to make the plans final, was staffed again by the Director of Operations. The approach shifted back to that of the first meeting; the staff was less directive and the action orientation less radical. Complaints were reiterated and an argument constructed to support the citizens' recommendations. But beyond the "strategy of rhetoric," there were no plans to mobilize a show of power in the event that the recommendations were not accepted.

[4] Peter Marris and Martin Rein, *Dilemmas of Social Reform* (New York: Atherton Press, 1967), pp. 176–181.

Clients or Constituents

Although personal preference was one factor determining the differences in approach between the Director of Operations and Director of Research, those differences may also be explained, in part, by the functions of the two positions within the MCHR. The Operations Division is responsible for building programs, which involves developing a symbiotic relationship with the delegate agencies. Hence, its Director is predisposed to ironing out differences through a cooperative approach. The Research Division, on the other hand, is responsible for evaluating programs, which predisposes it to a more critical approach and makes its relationship with delegate agencies less symbiotic. No division or person at the MCHR had community organization as its formal function.

The third person to enter the leadership cycle was the Executive Director of the MCHR, who acted as the main staff person in the session between the citizens and the Board of Education. A few minutes prior to this session, he met with the citizens and, acting as an advocate, made a number of suggestions on how the meeting might be conducted, what the citizens might ask for in addition to their program recommendations, and what action might be taken in the event that these requests were denied. But when the meeting commenced, his role shifted completely to that of an arbitrator. Standing between the Board of Education, with whom the MCHR had contracted for over a million dollars' worth of programs, and the citizens, to whom the MCHR was responsible by federal mandate, he took a nonpartisan position rather than run the risk of alienating one of the agency's major constituents. In effect, the citizens were without professional support during this meeting.

Throughout the confederation process, the MCHR endeavored to meet the demands of two incompatible masters. Thus, its role fluctuated between that of the arbitrator attempting to create a nonpartisan framework within which the conflicting interests of its constituents might be resolved, and that of an advocate attempting to strengthen the voice of the people. The end result was, inevitably, a leadership marked by confusion and indecision. The neighborhood representatives were never quite sure of the extent to

Confederated Action

which the MCHR would back them—whether, in the face of conflict, the MCHR would defend the citizens' interests or abandon the fight. Indeed, on these points, the MCHR itself was not sure.

Concluding a penetrating analysis of the community-action movement in the United States, Peter Marris and Martin Rein state: "No movement of reform in American society can hope to supplant the conflicts of interests from which policy evolves. It can only act as an advocate, not as a judge. If it is to be persuasive, it must be single-minded about the interest it represents, and so willing to surrender any claim to universal authority."[5] In sponsoring the citizens' confederation, the MCHR took a step in the direction of institutional reform, but was unwilling to surrender its "claim to universal authority." Organized without a firm sense of purpose and bred in ambiguity and indecision, the confederation had little foundation for a sustained effort.

FOLLOW-UP

More than two months after the meeting with the Board of Education, only one of the six neighborhood representatives was cognizant of the actual steps that had been taken to implement citizen recommendations. During this period, the citizens had made no effort to pursue the issue as a city-wide group, and the MCHR had made no attempt to inspire the confederation to launch a follow-up campaign.

Meanwhile, the Board of Education had made no decision concerning the Kindergarten Aide program, but it did submit to the MCHR a new job description for the School-Community Agents. In reference to this position, the citizens had made four specific requests: to have staff screened by the neighborhood personnel committees; to make the job qualifications more flexible so that nonprofessionals could hold these positions; to emphasize recruitment of pre-primary youth as the major function of the job; and, in general, to make the School-Community Agent more responsive to the community. The new job description contained no

[5] Marris and Rein, p. 230.

123

mention of neighborhood participation in the hiring process; the job qualifications eliminated the possibility of nonprofessional staff; and, under a section headed "Duties and Responsibilities," only the words "help recruit" referred obliquely to the recruitment of pre-primary youth. All this reflected the fact that, although received after the June meeting with the citizens, the job description was actually written at least one month before that meeting (it was attached to a memorandum circulated among Board of Education staff, dated April 26, 1967).

A few weeks after the new job description was received, the Executive Director of the MCHR sent a letter to the Superintend-ent of Schools requesting some action on the citizen recommenda-tions. He noted that the job description for the School-Community Agent did "not contain the ingredients requested by the citizens" and ended with the reminder that "we [MCHR] have a commit-ment to the citizens that matters of concern to them will be re-solved prior to the granting of OEO funds to a delegate agency."[6] The implication here was that the MCHR might use its power to invoke economic sanctions.

However, a week before this letter was sent, the antipoverty budget for the fiscal year 1967–1968 had been approved by the MCHR Board of Directors, and a certain percentage of it was thereby earmarked for Board of Education programs. Consequently, the possibility of imposing serious economic sanctions was signifi-cantly diminished. Once the budget was approved, the money could not be used to develop or support other than approved programs. At this point, if the MCHR wanted to impose economic sanctions, it could withhold funds, but not reallocate them. In light of the "something is better than nothing" psychology to which both staff and citizens generally subscribed, the viability of this alternative was somewhat questionable.

The Board of Education responded to Mr. Hill's letter in a seemingly positive manner. They decided to fund the Kindergarten

[6] Letter from David G. Hill, Executive Director, Mayor's Committee on Human Resources, Inc., July 12, 1967.

Confederated Action

Aide program under their Elementary and Secondary Education Act budget. As for the School-Community Agent program, the MCHR was informed that "the job description remains under study, and we will be glad to have your suggestions as to ways this role can be most effective to both the schools and the community."[7] Although the requests concerning hiring practices and job qualifications were not granted, the issue was subsequently resolved by an agreement that the School-Community Agents would operate, at least part time, out of the neighborhood centers.

In this follow-up, the MCHR exercised "paper pressure" rather than "people pressure." The letter sent to the Superintendent of Schools was direct, but not forceful; it reiterated the citizens' recommendations, but made no demands such as setting a deadline date for resolution of issues. It implied the use of economic sanctions, but the feasibility of actually invoking these sanctions had, for the most part, already been pre-empted. More important was the effect of this action on future citizen participation. The follow-up process was not congruent with the development of a powerful and independent citizens' confederation. Instead of taking steps to mobilize the confederation for pressure on the Board of Education, the MCHR assumed the role of an arbitrator attempting to settle a dispute between two of its constituents. Although an arbitrator may pass judgment, he can, at the same time, remain aloof, dispassionate, and neutral. Not only was this course of action safe in that it preserved the MCHR's neutrality, but writing a letter was also less demanding than organizing meetings and planning with citizens.

CITIZEN INFLUENCE

This case study suggests that the MCHR staff, while privately committed to the idea of creating an independent citizens' confederation capable of exerting forceful influence upon delegate agencies, has been unable to translate this private sentiment into

[7] Letter from Sidney Marland, Superintendent, Pittsburgh Public Schools, July 28, 1967.

125

an effective public course of action.[8] Foremost among the contributing factors were: the absence of internal coordination, the reluctance to abdicate a nonpartisan position, and the lack of a coherent strategy oriented toward the use of power. But the onus of this failure was not on staff alone; the citizens approached the confederation with a timid and parochial attitude which, under the best of circumstances, would be a constraint to unified action. Yet despite these shortcomings, the Board of Education did not ignore the citizens' recommendations; they agreed to refund the Kindergarten Aide program and proposed some changes in the School-Community Agent program.

Given these results, two questions remain to be answered: Did the citizens influence the final outcome? If so, how? In attempting to discern the impact of citizen participation, a few points about the Board of Education must be considered. First, the Board's final decisions were not essentially in opposition to its own interests. On the contrary, the Kindergarten Aides were recognized as valuable paraprofessional supports by the school principals and the kindergarten teachers, as well as by the central staff. The primary objection to refunding this program related to a presumed choice between eliminating professional or nonprofessional positions, and since the Kindergarten Aides were nonprofessionals, they would have lower priority than regular professional staff. As it turned out, the Board was able to keep the Kindergarten Aides without dismissing any professional employees, but they did make a subse-

---

[8] In discussing the role of Community Action Agencies, Herbert Gans points out: "Although one can argue that if poverty is to be reduced, the action agencies must . . . side with the clients and develop programs that will increase their economic and political role, the agencies cannot help but respond first to the sources of present power. Since most of the power is held by the 'establishment,' moral imperatives and programmatic necessities are of lower priority." He suggests: "What will probably happen is that the action agencies will side with the poor when they can and when the issue is not of great political significance, but the rest of the time they will side with those who have power in the community, meanwhile making it look as if they were on the side of the poor." Herbert Gans, "Urban Poverty and Social Planning," *The Uses of Sociology*, ed. Paul Lazarsfeld, William Sewell, and Harold Wilensky (New York: Basic Books, 1967), p. 460.

quent cutback in another category of nonprofessional staff. In so doing, the Board was able to protect its own interests (keeping professional staff) and at the same time react in a seemingly positive manner to the citizen recommendations (by responding to the specific content, if not the actual spirit, of these recommendations). Different was the fate of the citizen recommendations involving real changes in the status quo, those which were more incompatible with the Board's interests than was the Kindergarten Aide program —such as downgrading the qualifications for the School-Community Agent and involving neighborhood personnel committees in staff selection. These recommendations were summarily rejected.

A second factor to be considered in evaluating citizen influence is that the Pittsburgh Board of Education, like most school boards, is particularly sensitive about its public image. When it has an opportunity to make concessions that do not affect basic interests, as in this instance, it would be out of character for the Board not to use it to the best advantage. This is not to suggest that the Board was insincere in its desire to cooperate with the citizens or to have the best possible program; however, cooperation (which, incidentally, contributes to a favorable public image) is easier when interests coincide and no real sacrifices have to be made. A final factor is that, prior to the meeting with the citizens, the Board had indicated that it probably would not be able to refund the Kindergarten Aide program, and had indicated no plans to alter the School-Community Agent program. In answer to the first question, then, it is plausible to assume that the citizens did influence the Board's decisions, but that this influence was primarily on nonbasic issues that did not substantially change Board priorities.

This case, although only an initial attempt to organize citizen participation with a city-wide focus, provides a clear example of citizen influence on institutional decision-making throughout the brief history of the Pittsburgh Community Action Program. This influence has been based upon creating a climate of public opinion. It is particularly effective when citizen opinion and institutional interests do not clash; it is the type of influence more akin to that exercised in ratification than to that exercised in decision-making.

Clients or Constituents

As long as the MCHR continues to arbitrate rather than advocate, this form of influence seems to represent the upper limit of citizen participation attainable under its sponsorship. Although this is certainly a legitimate form of influence, it falls far short of the sharing in planning and decision-making envisioned by the MCHR staff at the outset of its efforts.

CHAPTER VII

The Opposition

$\mathbb{E}$arlier it was suggested that the War on Poverty can be characterized as a "peculiar" social movement, one that, while committed to social change, evokes only moderate opposition because its fundamental ideology is congruent with prevailing societal values. When applied to the antipoverty movement in its broadest aspect, this thesis appears to have general validity. In 1964 the movement was launched with the initial funding of ten Community Action Agencies. Less than four years later, 1,018 such agencies were in existence. The expeditious legislative passage

129

of this program and its rapid expansion through the use of federal funds could not have taken place without societal sanctions.[1] Yet, in various localities throughout the nation, the War on Poverty has experienced at least enough opposition to challenge the legitimacy of the local Community Action Agency and, in some cases, actually to abort the program's development. Therefore, although the general proposition of congruent societal values may account for the reaction to this movement on an overall national level, it is important to understand the dynamics that operate to facilitate or impede the movement's progress in particular cities. To help explain these dynamics, four key potential sources of local opposition were studied in Pittsburgh—the general public, the community leaders, the target agencies, and the target population.

PUBLIC IMAGE

One potential and significant source of opposition is the general public—the average middle-class citizens who are not directly involved with the program, but whose opinions, when strongly voiced, often shape public life. Whether these citizens support, oppose, or simply ignore the antipoverty movement depends upon how they perceive it: Does it present a challenge to the established order? Is it a dole to the poor or an attempt at self-help? And, perhaps most important, is its major objective to change the community, which might involve a reallocation of power and resources, or to change the individual? Members of the general public have few opportunities to observe the program directly as it operates. Their interpretations of the program are based, for the most part, on information channeled through the mass media. Thus, the image created by the mass media, regardless of its validity, may substantially influence the manner in which the War on Poverty effort on both the local and the national level is perceived.

[1] With regard to the passage of the Economic Opportunity Act of 1964, one prominent authority suggests that no single piece of domestic legislation of comparable importance had moved so rapidly and easily through Congress in a quarter of a century. See John C. Donovan, *The Politics of Poverty* (New York: Pegasus, 1967), p. 37.

The Opposition

In an effort to capture the image of the Pittsburgh program, 140 newspaper articles published over a period of fifteen months were analyzed. They appeared between March 1966 and May 1967 in the *Pittsburgh Press* and the *Pittsburgh Post Gazette,* the city's two major newspapers. These articles focused upon events and activities explicitly identified as part of the local antipoverty program. During this period, a number of articles appeared on the activities of groups that were related to the antipoverty program but were not specifically identified as such; these articles are not included in the present analysis, but will be discussed later.

As Table 5 indicates, the articles were divided into three

Table 5

NEWSPAPER COVERAGE OF THE PITTSBURGH ANTIPOVERTY
PROGRAM, MARCH 1966–MAY 1967

Image	Service	Citizen Participation	General Information	Total
Positive	52% (72)	13% (18)	18% (25)	83% (115)
Negative	5% (8)	12% (17)	0% (0)	17% (25)
Total	57% (80)	25% (35)	18% (25)	100% (140)

categories based upon their content—whether related primarily to service aspects of the program, to citizen participation, or to general information. Within each category the articles were judged as projecting either a positive or a negative image of the program. Those rated as positive generally contained stories of success, cooperation, self-help, individual change, or praise by an outsider. The content of these articles was reflected in headlines such as: "Youth Projects Keep Poor Busy," "Retraining 'Ineligibles' to Get Help," and " 'Self-Help' South Oakland Topic." Those articles judged as presenting a negative image noted failure, internal bickering, protest, conflict with established institutions, or censure by an outsider. Here the content was presented under headings such as: "Poverty War Eye Test Ripped; Optometrists Denied Role," "Pov-

131

erty Plan Rejected in Strip; Near Violence at Meeting," and "What to Cut Stirs Battle Over Schools."

The predominant newspaper image of the Pittsburgh War on Poverty is one of a benign, service-oriented program. As the data indicate, more than one-half of the articles covered service aspects of the program, one-fourth reported citizen-participation activities, and less than one-fourth focused upon general information; over 80 per cent of these articles described aspects of the program that generally did not reflect an adverse image. This image is somewhat exaggerated, although not altogether distorted. It is an image that the MCHR worked hard to maintain, and one that the local press bought on face value without probing very much beneath the surface. A more accurate, and perhaps to many a less favorable, picture of the Pittsburgh program would not substantially alter the emphasis on service that was projected by the press; but it would modify somewhat the bright colors of success in which these services were painted, it would admit to more internal conflict, and it would recognize the scope and subtleties of "negative" citizen activities.

A number of reasons explain the extremely benign image projected by the Pittsburgh program. Foremost is the fact that the MCHR, following normative organizational patterns, was disinclined to reveal its backstage behavior to the public. Whenever a potentially controversial topic was placed on the MCHR Board's agenda, an "executive session" was called, which was a relatively diplomatic way to exclude the press and public from the meeting. Also, the MCHR was hesitant to identify itself with the more radical citizens' groups, even though antipoverty personnel and resources invariably supported such efforts behind the scenes or in the neighborhoods. Between March 1966 and May 1967, over twenty articles appeared in the local press, covering the activities of these groups, under such headings as: "East Street Citizens Vow to Delay Road"; "Northside Slum Battle Grows as Both Sides Win New Allies"; and "Marchers Demand Higher Grants." In these articles, the MCHR, OEO, or the generic "Pittsburgh antipoverty program" was rarely mentioned, and was never directly identified

132

The Opposition

with the citizen efforts. This omission occurred despite the facts that: some members of the MCHR Board were key figures in many of these activities; meetings were recurrently held in anti-poverty offices; antipoverty resources, including mimeograph machines, typewriters, paper, and secretarial staff, were used in abundance; antipoverty staff were actively involved in organizing these efforts; and many of the citizens and organizations directly affiliated with the MCHR were officially sponsoring these efforts.

Finally, the press itself took something less than a critical approach toward the program. Rarely did it attempt to delve beneath the surface; reports of successful ventures often reflected only the "better side of reality"; success usually was judged according to the number game—if many people were being contacted, served, or put to work, a program was reported as "successful"; no connection was made between the more radical social action activities and the overall antipoverty enterprise. The quality, purpose, or final outcome of a service or activity was seldom questioned.

COMMUNITY LEADERS

Early in 1967, a study was conducted by an outside agency to determine the effects of the War on Poverty in Pittsburgh. Part of the study involved detailed interviews with about twenty-five community leaders. They were selected on the basis of their knowledge of, and influence in, the community and included individuals such as: elected local officials, heads of local government agencies, directors of voluntary organizations, members of the press, civil rights leaders, and business executives. The study concluded that "a large majority of the community leaders hold highly favorable views of the OEO Community Action Program in Pittsburgh" and that, with few exceptions, the community leaders are more generous than the MCHR staff in their estimates of the program's successes.[2]

[2] Daniel Yankelovich, Inc., *Evaluation of the Pittsburgh, Pennsylvania Community Action Program,* Prepared for the Office of Economic Opportunity (May 1967), p. 22. For a more detailed report of this study see, Daniel Yankelovich, Inc., *Detailed Findings of Study to Determine Effects of CAP Programs on Selected Communities and Their Low-Income*

Clients or Constituents

Why this favorable reception accorded by community leaders to the Pittsburgh antipoverty program? One respondent suggested that the way the program was set up partially accounts for its success. He noted that "everyone sat down together to plan it. As a result, everyone was in on it and no one had a vested interest."[3] In actuality, not everyone was involved in the planning; as Chapter III indicates, the poor never seriously participated in the program's development. Furthermore, the idea that because "everyone" was involved no one had a vested interest is patently questionable. It is more likely that this respondent was trying to suggest that, because everyone was involved, no one's vested interests were either endangered or distinctly advantaged. Nevertheless, in mentioning planning, involvement, and vested interests, this respondent did hit upon the raw ingredients making for a favorable reception.

The initial plans for the program were developed mainly by those who had the most in the way of immediate vested interests to protect: the local welfare organizations. It is not difficult to understand why, quite early in the planning process, it was decided that the program be built upon available resources, that is, those of the local welfare organizations. When the program was officially launched, leaders from various other segments of the community were on the MCHR Board, which was initially composed of members representing the Mellon Family, the Pittsburgh National Bank, labor, the Catholic Diocese, civil rights, the Health and Welfare Council, and the city administration. The whole process, from planning to implementation, was realized under the firm guidance of the mayor's office. Thus, in establishing the program, a coalition of interests was developed, comprehensive in scope and almost immune to attack. If the community leaders in Pittsburgh are inclined to view the city's antipoverty program favorably, it is largely because, from the outset, their interests were well-represented. The

Residents, Prepared for the Office of Economic Opportunity (March 1967), pp. 145–217.

[3] Daniel Yankelovich, Inc., *Evaluation of the Pittsburgh, Pennsylvania Community Action Program,* Prepared for the Office of Economic Opportunity (May 1967), p. 23.

The Opposition

program, by the very composition of its planning and policy-making staff, did not present much of a threat to the established order.

However, people react not only to things that threaten them. As indicated in the discussion of its public image, the program was seen by many as providing real opportunities for self-help and individual improvement. Some of the community leaders perceived the program's benefits in terms of social control, particularly with regard to racial violence. The provision of services was also considered an important benefit. Others saw the program as providing a medium of communication drawing different groups closer together. Most of the respondents were not dissatisfied with the degree and type of citizen participation—and of those who were, few suggested that the poor should have greater influence or control over the program.[4]

TARGET AGENCIES

So far, the discussion has been concerned with opposition, or rather the lack of opposition, emanating from the general public and community leaders. Both, however, are removed from the program; they rarely see it in operation or feel its effects—unlike the welfare system and the target population. The third potential source of opposition is grounded much closer to the battlefield, that is, among the members of participating agencies, particularly those staff who daily man the front lines and provide both ammunition and target for the antipoverty efforts. These welfare personnel are in the awkward position of simultaneously supplying the antipoverty forces with services and protecting their agency's autonomy against encroachment by these very same forces.

The participating agencies have little reason to oppose supplying services to the War on Poverty. On the contrary, supplying services is their business, and they, like most enterprises, welcome new markets and growth, especially when the financial rewards are to be so quickly reaped. Herein lies one reason that these staff and agencies, although vulnerable, have not raised any serious complaints against the program—the incentives seem to far outweigh

[4] Daniel Yankelovich.

135

the risks. The incentives are related not only to expansion through a new federally subsidized market, but also to the fact that this market has substantially altered salary scales for a number of service professions, social work and education being the two affected most. In Pittsburgh, the participating agencies generally supported the service aspects of the program; and, aside from a few isolated incidents, their reactions to citizen participation were far from hostile, although there was an underlying current of suspicion and opposition, as the case study in Chapter VI suggests.

However, the economic incentive to participate provides only a partial explanation for this lack of opposition. A more complete explanation involves the attitudes and perceptions of agency staff concerning citizen involvement and its consequences—particularly those staff in administrative positions who were responsible for direct dealings with citizens' groups. As the data in Table 6 sug-

Table 6

AGENCY STAFF PERCEPTION OF THE REASON
FOR CITIZEN PARTICIPATION ($N = 26$)

Primary Reason for Participation	*Staff Members (Percentage)*
To increase the influence of the poor	11.5
To allow the poor to express their needs	34.6
To achieve better interaction between agencies and the poor	38.5
To educate the poor for self-help	15.4
Total	100

gest, the vast majority of administrative staff at this level did not perceive citizen participation primarily as a vehicle for increasing the influence of the poor upon the agencies that serve them; instead, they considered its most important function to be the less threatening and disruptive one of facilitating communications.

The Opposition

When asked to describe the actual impact of citizen participation upon program development, the respondents more or less split down the middle. About one-half viewed citizen influence as slight or indirect, whereas the other half perceived citizens as directly molding programs, either through external pressure against opponents or as partners in the decision-making process. Although 80 per cent of the respondents were dissatisfied with the results of citizen participation, very few expressed concern that the citizens had too much influence, too little influence, or the wrong kind of influence over the program. Most were disturbed by the quantitative paucity of low-income participants.

Overall, these data suggest three factors relevant to understanding the lack of agency opposition. First, the staff responsible for dealing with citizens, for the most part, did not perceive the primary function of citizen participation as threatening their autonomy. Second, the divided opinion concerning the actual impact of citizen participation supports the idea (outlined in Chapters V and VI) that there were few clear-cut instances of forceful citizen influence in the decision-making arena. If this were not the case, it is unlikely that one-half of the front-line administrative staff would have characterized citizen influence as slight or otherwise indirect, since it is easier to attribute influence in a situation in which it is not clearly discernible than to deny its existence in one where it is forcibly applied. For example, if on a specific issue, citizen and agency interests coincide, as they frequently do, one might claim that the citizens prevailed, whereas in reality there was no contention to begin with. Finally, these staff and the agencies they represented were committed to the program not only out of self-serving motives for an economic gain that provided little threat to their autonomy, but also because it seemed to offer a new and creative opportunity to attack the social ills of the day. If many of them were not anxious to share decision-making authority with the neighborhood councils, they at least wanted to establish a dialogue with those they served. The agency staff were dissatisfied with citizen participation because they did not consider the neighborhood boards as qualitatively or quantitatively representative of their client population, and the dialogue they desired was thereby not facilitated.

Another, and in some cases the most potent, source of opposition emanates from the target population itself, which was demonstrated in Pittsburgh by the brief but fierce struggle that racked the Lawrenceville community when the program was first being organized (the Lawrenceville experience is discussed in Chapter IV). This incident, however, was an exception. For the most part, the citizen participants in Pittsburgh accepted the program with equanimity, which was illustrated, among other things, by the fact that citizens rarely criticized the MCHR in public even though its board functioned for more than a year without representation of the poor.

The lack of citizen opposition may be attributed partially to the utilization of citizen-staff interpersonal relationships. In six of the eight antipoverty neighborhoods, the coordination contracts went to agencies that had been in the community-organization business prior to the War on Poverty. In most of these neighborhoods, strong interpersonal bonds between staff and citizens were already established. Such relationships also existed with some of the key figures "downtown." Morton Coleman of the mayor's office, and Kiernan Stenson, the Director of Operations for the MCHR, both had extensive contacts in the neighborhoods prior to the antipoverty program. These relationships produced an element of trust and good faith that worked against the emergence of serious opposition by the citizen participants.

Pittsburgh's relatively quick success in obtaining antipoverty funds and its national acclaim as a model program also served to inhibit opposition. People enjoy being identified with a successful operation and can tolerate certain faults better if it is perceived as such. The accomplishments of the Pittsburgh program led citizen participants to repress dissatisfaction because, even if the program was not perfect, it was certainly thought better than most. Also, the citizens were as anxious as the MCHR to maintain the model pro-

The Opposition

gram reputation and to reap the federally subsidized rewards that accompanied it. In addition, the program itself provided the citizens with direct benefits that committed them to its support. The antipoverty neighborhood boards were officially recognized by the MCHR as the voice of the community. Membership on these boards held certain status connotations derived from this relationship with the MCHR. Hence, a challenge to the MCHR's legitimacy was at the same time a threat to the status of the neighborhood board members. Moreover, the program presented an opportunity for economic mobility through the creation of subprofessional positions. The citizens were not anxious to endanger these opportunities for status and mobility by being overly critical of the program or its leadership.

BROADER CONTEXT

As the preceding discussion indicates, opposition to the development and expansion of Pittsburgh's antipoverty movement was generally negligible. There were a few short-lived incidents, but aside from the elusive and subtle forms of opposition that are difficult to uncover and more difficult to document, there was no organized long-range effort of any consequence aimed at undermining or deprecating the Pittsburgh program. The reasons for this phenomenon are obviously varied and complex, and causes and effects are not easily untangled. Although conscious efforts were made to create the ingredients for harmony, certain unique features of the city's history and circumstances also played an important role.

The city's relatively successful experience with urban renewal set a precedent for the creation of a stable and strong coalition of community leaders. It also provided a comprehensive network of institutional and personal linkages through which this coalition could be rapidly activated. The ACTION-Housing Neighborhood Urban Extension Program helped to develop citizen-staff relationships in what later became antipoverty neighborhoods and provided a model for neighborhood participation that was based, in part, upon the principle of interagency cooperation. Thus some of the potential friction points in the development of the antipoverty program were already well oiled. In addition, the mayor's firm support, coupled with the monolithic political structure of the city, preempted intergovernmental struggles that embroiled politically less homogeneous cities. The absence of militant civil rights organizations allowed for a swift and peaceful settlement with the Negro community. And the presence of skilled and sophisticated urban technicians facilitated the overall process of intergroup cooperation that marked the program's development.

CHAPTER VIII

Internal Solidarity

$\mathbb{I}$n preceding chapters, the terms *participant, citizen, neighborhood representative,* and *the poor* have been used synonymously except where otherwise designated. The implication has been that, for the most part, those who participate on neighborhood councils represent a particular socioeconomic interest group —one which has lain dormant but which might be stimulated by professionals to exert influence upon local institutions that mold the environmental life-space of the poor. The poor, with professional help, were to be transformed from clients to constituents.

Clients or Constituents

For this transformation to occur, the interest group, whether labeled the poor, the citizens, or neighborhood representatives, must be of such nature that collective action is possible. The members of the group must possess certain social-psychological attributes that predispose them to cooperate in a collective venture. The presence or absence of these attributes determines the potential for achieving internal solidarity. It has been suggested (in Chapter II) that the development of internal solidarity is based on three essential elements: congruent membership, group identification, and common ideology. To the degree that any one or a combination of these elements is lacking, the ability to achieve collective action is diminished.

Internal solidarity in the Pittsburgh antipoverty movement is discussed here in terms of the attributes of neighborhood council board members—whether they facilitate or impede collective action in pursuit of the movement's objectives. Although individuals other than board members participate on the neighborhood level, the analysis includes only board members because of the structure of representation in the neighborhoods and because of the relative power and influence of the boards; they are the bodies that almost always initiate, process, and ratify antipoverty actions emanating in the name of citizen participation.

REPRESENTATION

Before analyzing the membership of Pittsburgh's neighborhood council boards for congruency with the objectives of citizen participation, the representational structure of these bodies must be considered. The idea of representation covers a broad spectrum, ranging from the self-appointed and often demagogic champion of a highly specific interest group to the democratically elected political representative of the "people"; in between, there are many arrangements, each varying in the degree and type of responsibility that the representative has to the group he represents. For example, there are those who are adjudged representative by informal group consensus; those who are appointed to represent a group by non-group members; those who are selected or elected because they provide representation for two or more groups at the same time (such as the non-neighborhood members of the MCHR Board who were chosen because of formal connections with welfare agency boards and informal ties with the establishment); and those who are selected by the group they represent, but whose selection must be ratified by nongroup members (such as the citizen representatives of the MCHR Board). Wilbur Newstetter's typology of intergroup representational structures provides the basis for a clear, if somewhat simplified, illustration of the relationship between representational structure and congruent membership. This scheme contains three types of intergroup representation:[1] *Type I*—Members are official delegates, elected or appointed by the groups they represent, and may act only upon the group's instruction. *Type II*—Members are official delegates, elected or appointed by the groups they represent, and are more or less free to act independently in the group's interest. *Type III*—Members are selected, appointed, or recognized on the basis of certain attributes as representative of a group by other than members of that group, and are not formally responsible to their supposed constituents.

If the membership on the neighborhood council boards reflected a Type I or a Type II representational structure, then the question of congruent membership would be addressed not to the individual board members, but to the entire group or constituency that they officially represent. Here the board members would be responsible to the groups that elected or appointed them, and that have the ultimate recourse of recalling them; thus, the personal attributes of the representatives have little relevance to the question of whom they represent. In Type I and Type II structures, for example, Negroes can represent whites or Catholics can represent Jews, if the groups so choose. The OEO regulation concerning representation of the poor further illustrates this setup. It states: "Such representatives need not themselves be poor, but they must be se-

[1] Wilbur I. Newstetter, "The Social Inter-Group Work Process: How Does It Differ from Social Group Work Process?" *Community Organization: Its Nature and Setting*, ed. Donald S. Howard (New York: American Association of Social Workers, 1947), pp. 26–27.

lected in a manner that insures that they truly represent the poor."[2] The selection process here implies a Type I or Type II structure that few antipoverty programs have achieved; even in cities (such as Philadelphia) where neighborhood elections were a relatively elaborate affair in terms of time and money, the turnout at election time (less than 3 per cent of eligible voters) barely reflected the "voice of the people."[3] This result comes as no surprise, as the inter-relationship between poverty and political apathy has been analyzed frequently as more than a matter of coincidence.[4]

However, in the Type III structure, the personal attributes of the representatives are the primary criteria of their representativeness. Here the representatives are chosen by other than the members of their supposed constituency; the assumption is that if their personal characteristics are similar to those of a particular group, their actions will reflect the attitudes and interests of this group. The lines of responsibility between these representatives and their constituencies are much more vague and informal than in the Type I and Type II structures.[5]

Which of these structures do the neighborhood council boards in Pittsburgh most closely approximate? The MCHR, in

[2] Office of Economic Opportunity, CAP Memo No. 57, January 11, 1967, p. 3.

[3] In Philadelphia, organized slates backed by settlement houses, the NAACP, local civic clubs, and local political clubs succeeded in electing a majority of the community's twelve council members. For a relatively non-critical description of the election experience in this city, see Arthur B. Shostak, "Promoting Participation of the Poor: Philadelphia's Anti-Poverty Program," *Social Work*, 1966, *11*(1), 73–80.

[4] For a discussion of this interrelationship, see Warren C. Haggstrom, "The Power of the Poor," *Mental Health of the Poor*, ed. Frank Riessman, Jerome Cohen, Arthur Pearl (New York: Free Press, 1964), pp. 205–223.

[5] Prior to the OEO mandate that representatives of the poor be democratically elected, it was suggested that "when representatives are not available, or insufficient in number, an alternative strategy is to appoint to board positions individuals drawn from the poverty population who do not necessarily represent local organizations, but who can serve as interpreters of the poor. These are individuals sufficiently familiar with the unorganized poor that they can effectively speak in their behalf." Office of Economic Opportunity, Resident Participation, January 28, 1965, p. 7 (mimeographed).

outlining the criteria for the official neighborhood antipoverty units, emphasized that the board members be representative of the neighborhoods in terms of specific status characteristics, but not that they be democratically determined. While many of the neighborhoods went through some vague form of an election process, the slate of candidates was generally developed by the local coordinating agencies, and the turnouts at "election time" rarely approached 2 per cent of any neighborhood's population. The vagueness of the election processes is substantiated by the fact that once elected, selected, or appointed, the majority (56 per cent) of board members did not perceive themselves as representing the interests of any particular constituency (see Table 7). From these factors one must conclude

Table 7

PERCEPTIONS OF GROUP REPRESENTATION
BY NEIGHBORHOOD BOARD MEMBERS (*N*=*256*)

Groups Represented	*Board Members (Percentage)*
None	56
Geographic (neighborhood)	8
Economic (both the poor and the middle class)	16
Other[a]	16
No information	4
Total	100

[a] This category includes racial groups, ethnic groups, religious groups, and institutional groups.

that Pittsburgh's neighborhood council boards most closely approximate the Type III structure of representation.

Because of the Type III setup, the degree of correspondence between the membership and the participatory objectives of Pittsburgh's antipoverty program is primarily a function of the personal attributes of those who represent and make decisions in behalf of the poor. This is true whether the objective of citizen participation is viewed as a mechanism for promoting participatory democracy for the poor, or as a mechanism for promoting individual change through involvement in community affairs, or as some combination of the two; in any case, the attributes of the representatives must to a high degree resemble those of a broad cross-section of the poor. This resemblance would not exist in a Type I or Type II structure, where the poor might elect nonpoor individuals to represent their interests; if the nonpoor representatives did not act in these interests, they could be recalled. The poverty constituency has no such power in a Type III structure.

STATUS ATTRIBUTES

An analysis of congruent membership in the antipoverty movement might cover a number of theoretically relevant attributes; what is covered depends upon how one defines the poor. Most definitions of the poor as a group emphasize either class characteristics, especially income and education, or cultural characteristics, such as style of life.[6] Both the cultural and the class perspectives are incorporated in the following analysis, which attempts to determine how closely the characteristics of neighborhood board members resemble those of the poor. Three cultural indicators are employed, based on utilization of welfare services, participation in voluntary organizations, and perceptions of economic mobility. The use of these three indicators was based on the assumption that the poor may be characterized, for the most part, as clients of the welfare system, as economically immobile, and (with the exception of the antipoverty movement, in which conscious and professional efforts were made to elicit participation) as nonparticipants in volun-

---

[6] For an effort at welding "class" and "cultural" characteristics to describe better the diversity that exists in the poverty population, see S. M. Miller, "The American Lower Classes: A Typological Approach," *New Perspectives on Poverty,* ed. Arthur Shostak and William Gomberg (Englewood Cliffs, N.J.: Prentice-Hall, 1965), pp. 22–39. Herbert Gans in *The Urban Villagers* (New York: Free Press, 1962), pp. 229–278, presents a style of life description of the poor.

tary organizations. Thus, to the degree that neighborhood board members exhibit these attributes, they may, from a cultural perspective, be considered more or less representative of the poor.

The data contained in Table 8 and 9 suggest that few of the neighborhood board members possess the cultural characteristics of the poor. First, over a two and one-half year period of time, the vast majority of board members did not use any of the services provided by the antipoverty program. Of those who did use them, about one-fourth used only one education service, usually involving supplementary education for their children; fewer than one-fourth of the consumers used more than one service. The emerging picture, which hardly resembles that of a consumer-client population, presents a somewhat curious circumstance in light of the fact that neighborhood boards are charged with the responsibility for planning and evaluating antipoverty services, mainly on the supposition that they represent the consumer-client group. Second, the board members do not seem characteristic of the alienated, nonparticipating segments of the community. On the contrary, they are, by an overwhelming margin, the joiners; prior to the antipoverty movement, they belonged to civil rights groups, church organizations, PTAs, block clubs, civic groups, ethnic associations, and other types of voluntary organizations.[7] Finally, the board members are distinguished from the poor in that they are an upwardly mobile group —or so they claim. Using Table 9 a simple index may be constructed employing cells 1, 2, and 3 to indicate economic mobility; cells 4, 5, and 6 to indicate economic stability; and cells 7, 8, and 9 to indicate economic decline. Though admittedly crude, this index does suggest that about 66 per cent of the board members judge themselves to be moving up the economic ladder.

It is abundantly clear that, on the basis of perceived economic mobility, utilization of service, and participation, a large gap

---

[7] Examining the relationship between social class and participation, Murray Hausknecht concludes, "the results are unambiguous: No matter what index of social stratification is used, the higher the class position, the greater the rate of voluntary association membership." Hausknecht, *The Joiners* (New York: Bedminister Press, 1962), p. 17.

Table 8

PRIOR PARTICIPATION AND UTILIZATION OF SERVICES BY NEIGHBORHOOD BOARD MEMBERS ($N=256$) (Percentages)

	Membership in Voluntary Organizations Prior to the Antipoverty Program	Utilization of any Antipoverty Welfare Services
Yes	85.9[a]	27.7[b]
No	13.3	71.5
N/A	.8	.8
Total	100	100

[a] Of those 85.9 per cent board members who participated in voluntary organizations prior to the antipoverty program, about 34 per cent were members of organizations that had an institutional focus, such as Parent-Teacher Associations or church-related groups; about 13 per cent were members of organizations that have a community or ethnic focus such as block clubs, chambers of commerce, and ethnic associations; and about 39 per cent were members of more than one type of organization.

[b] Of those 27.7 per cent board members who were services users, about 7 per cent used an educational service, in most cases the Head Start Program for their children. About 14 per cent used some other single service. Only 6 per cent were multiple-service users.

Table 9

PERCEIVED ECONOMIC MOBILITY OF NEIGHBORHOOD BOARD MEMBERS ($N=251$)

Perceived Changes in Economic Conditions Over the Last Ten Years	Perceived Economic Conditions Relative to Parents (Percentages)			
	Better	Same	Worse	Total
Improved	42.2 (1)[a]	7.6 (2)	4.8 (4)	54.6
Same	15.9 (3)	13.9 (5)	5.6 (7)	35.4
Declined	2.8 (6)	2.8 (8)	4.4 (9)	10.0
Total	60.9	24.3	14.8	100

[a] The numbers in parentheses are used to designate cell blocks within the table, and are referred to as such in the previous discussion.

exists between the cultural characteristics of board members and those of the poor. This evidence, however, is not in itself sufficient to disclaim correspondence between the characteristics of board members and those of their constituency. It would still be possible and plausible for board members to constitute a middle-class-oriented segment of the low-income population; that is, the upwardly mobile poor who, in striving to break out of poverty, have adopted certain middle-class modes of behavior.[8] If this were the case, they would not be invalidated as Type III representatives; the notion that only the inarticulate, unmotivated, and apathetic "hard core" constitute the poor contradicts logic and disregards the diversity of this population. Although the style of life may differ among members of the low-income population, they still exist on the verge of want and have strong common interests to put forth and defend.

To round out the picture of the correspondence between the poor and neighborhood board members, the class characteristics of these members must be examined. One approach would be to dichotomize board members into "poor" and "nonpoor" categories based upon Office of Economic Opportunity criteria; this division, however, provides only a very gross picture which, for the purpose of analyzing congruent membership, deserves little more than a footnote.[9] Rather than attempting to compare the class characteristics of board members to some formal quantitative definition of poverty, the approach used here is to see how their characteristics relate to those of the resident population of the eight antipoverty neighborhoods in Pittsburgh. This approach is used for two reasons. First, it provides a relatively generous definition of the class characteristics of the poor. The antipoverty neighborhoods were chosen because, at least in gross statistical terms, they reflected the most depressed areas in the city; but, within each neighborhood, various gradations of social and economic well-being exist. Thus, the me-

---

[8] See Bernard Berelson and Gary A. Steiner, *Human Behavior* (New York: Harcourt, 1964), p. 487.

[9] Using the OEO index to determine poverty—built on the variables of family size and income, with a base of $1,500 for a one-person family and increasing by $500 for each additional family member—approximately 19 per cent of the neighborhood board members are poor.

dian neighborhood figures for certain class indicators represent a point between those residents in dire poverty and those residents whose socioeconomic condition might be characterized as that of the working class or the lower-middle class. Second, the Economic Opportunity Act of 1964, in outlining the requirements for "maximum feasible participation," speaks of involving both "residents of the areas and members of the groups served."

The class composition of neighborhood boards is, judging from the data in Table 10, not typical of the resident population. The data quite consistently suggest that the board members stand above their supposed constituents: they earn more money; they are more likely to own their own homes; and they are considerably more educated, with almost enough advanced degrees between them to start a small college. The amazingly high educational attainment of board members in part reflects the heavy participation of ministers, which in itself is a significant factor in considering congruent membership. Overall, the majority of neighborhood board members are homeowners with at least a high school education, earning more than $5,000 a year.

Further evidence along these lines may be gleaned from the board members' subjective evaluations of their social class positions. When polled on this question, the board members revealed that over one third of these people consider themselves at least middle class, and over one half think of themselves as belonging to the working class. Only a small fraction of the board members placed themselves in the lower-class category. Although self-estimated distinctions such as these are by no means precise, the social stratification of neighborhood boards reflected in these data appears to be relatively accurate in light of the objective characteristics.

The racial composition of neighborhood boards is another significant dimension of congruent membership. Although race does connote certain cultural and class characteristics, it is here treated as a separate category, since the issue is whether the board members exhibit characteristics not just of the poor, but of a board cross-section of the poverty population. To the extent that any one segment of this population is disproportionately represented on the

Internal Solidarity

Table 10

CLASS CHARACTERISTICS OF THE RESIDENT POPULATION
OF ANTIPOVERTY NEIGHBORHOODS AND OF MEMBERS
OF NEIGHBORHOOD COUNCIL BOARDS (*Percentages*)

		Board Members 1967	Residents 1960
Income:			
0–$1,999		10.9	16.4
$2,000–$2,999		8.5	10.5
$3,000–$3,999		7.8	12.9
$4,000–$4,999		10.9	15.4
$5,000 or more		57.0	44.8
	N/A	4.9	—
	Total	100	100
Home ownership:			
Own		55.9	38.5
Rent		43.4	61.5
	N/A	.7	—
	Total	100	100
Education:			
Some elementary school		3.1	31.1
Elementary school graduate		2.3	20.6
Some high school		18.8	24.2
High school graduate		27.0	18.4
Some college		23.4	3.2
College graduate		4.3	2.5[a]
Post-graduate work		19.5	—
	N/A	1.6	—
	Total	100	100

[a] This figure includes those who have studied four or more years in college.

boards, the total population base from which support for collective action may be drawn is likely to be similarly limited, and the movement's objectives are likely to become identified in terms of that subgroup's specific interests rather than in broader terms. The ques-

151

tion, then, is how closely does the racial composition of the neighborhood boards mirror that of their major potential constituency, the residential population of the antipoverty neighborhoods? The data in Table 11 show that, relative to the residential population,

Table 11

RACIAL COMPOSITION OF NEIGHBORHOOD BOARDS
(*Percentages*)

Race	Board Members 1967	Total Population of Antipoverty Neighborhoods 1960
Negro	61.7	33.8
White	37.5	66.2
N/A	.8	—
Total	100	100

a disproportionate number of board members are Negro; totaling about one-third of the neighborhood population, they comprise almost two-thirds of the board population. Overall, then, black persons have proportionately twice as much representation as white persons. The disparity becomes even greater when the figures are broken down by neighborhood. Almost two-thirds of the Negro residential population is concentrated in two neighborhoods, whose boards account for 22 per cent of the total Negro board members; hence, the other six neighborhoods average a Negro population of 11 per cent, while their boards average a 38 per cent Negro population. Thus broken down, black representation is proportionately about three-and-one-half times that of whites. These figures come as little surprise since, as suggested earlier, the Pittsburgh structure was developed in a manner that tended to identify the antipoverty program as a Negro movement.

Congruent membership does not lend itself to precise measurement. Nevertheless, inferential qualitative judgments are possible, using a variety of quantitative data. It is reasonable to infer from the data just presented that congruent membership is lacking in the Pittsburgh program. More specifically, there seems to be a low degree of correspondence between the objectives of the movement and the status attributes of its most active and most influential members. Even by a very liberal definition of "poor," the vast majority are not socioeconomically poor; an even larger majority do not exhibit the cultural characteristics of the poor; and the racial structure of the membership is not consistent with the involvement of a broad cross-section of the low-income population.

ATTITUDINAL CHARACTERISTICS

This lack of congruent membership implies that board members are not likely to act in the interest of the poor and, consequently, not likely to gain the collective support of the poor. However, this implication may not necessarily hold true or make collective action impossible. As William Cameron suggests: "The significance of social class membership is complicated. People who are really downtrodden do not often form political movements, or indeed anything, except escape movements. History has rarely recorded a successful slave revolt. Where movements have emerged representing the depressed classes in a society they have often as not been led by people of a higher social status, and financial support has often come from outside."[10]

Thus, the development of collective action also depends upon the extent to which the core leadership of any social movement, in this case the neighborhood board members, identifies with the group whose interests they ostensibly represent. When the leaders are drawn from a social stratum above that of their constituents, identification involves the ability to transcend one's own self-interests or the interests normally identified with one's social class. Identification is the psychological cement that may unite people of different status in a common cause. It is no simple matter to determine the extent to which neighborhood board members identify with the poor. The available evidence on this subject is far from

[10] William B. Cameron, *Modern Social Movements* (New York: Random House, 1966), p. 39.

complete; nevertheless, some clues exist. The phenomenon of group identification is examined from three perspectives, based upon data previously presented: class identification, representation, and neighborhood orientation.

First, the vast majority of board members do not view the lower class as their reference group; 50 per cent see themselves as working class and almost 40 per cent consider themselves as middle class or higher. This subjective sense of belonging to a class group has in itself certain implications, regardless of its validity as measured by objective class indicators. In studying the relationship between occupational status and subjective estimates of class standing, Richard Centers found that if people's class identifications are the same, their attitudes tend to be similar, even though their objective occupational positions are different.[11] Second, less than 16 per cent of the board members consider themselves as representing the interests of the poor; about one-half see themselves as representing no group; and the rest are divided among various ethnic, religious, and neighborhood groups. These figures suggest, at best, a weak sense of identification with the poor. Third, the parochial neighborhood orientation of board members (discussed in Chapter V) presents an alternative point of reference. Identification based upon residential status, even in a low-income neighborhood, is in all probability more attractive than identification with the poor, especially to those who come from the upwardly mobile low-income segments of the community. The contention that board members identify more strongly with their own locale and local organizations than with the poor is empirically substantiated by the events that occur during attempts at neighborhood federation. In viewing the evidence from these three perspectives, a cautious conclusion may be drawn that the poor are not a significant reference group for board members, the major citizen participants of Pittsburgh's antipoverty movement.

Up to this point, the discussion has centered around the

[11] Richard Centers, *The Psychology of Social Classes* (Princeton: Princeton University Press, 1949), pp. 125–140.

element of self-interest; it has considered the degree to which a commonality of self-interest exists between the leadership and the constituency of the Pittsburgh antipoverty movement, as reflected by both the social status and group identification of the leadership. People join together because of common self-interests; but unless they are imbued with common sets of attitudes, values, and beliefs, the group in which they collect is rarely able to act successfully in defense of its interests. Thus, whereas common self-interest forms a major basis for collection in a group, common ideology is the keystone of collective group action. Ideology, therefore, is a significant dimension of such a collective venture; it unites people of common cause in common action. As C. Wendell King notes, the ideology of a social movement provides a rationale "not only for the objectives but for the tactical and organization means to those objectives —it must make a good case for what the movement is trying to do and how it is trying to do it."[12] To the extent that members of a social movement adhere to a common ideology, the potential for collective action is enhanced.

The question arises: does a consensus exist among neighborhood board members about the ideology of citizen participation? More specifically, to what extent do these individuals hold a common view of citizen participation as a tactical means for achieving the democratization and reform of social welfare? Regarding this question, the data in Table 12 suggest a considerable discrepancy in board members' attitudes: almost one half of these individuals view citizen participation as a mechanism for facilitating communication between welfare agencies and the poor; an equal number see it as a mechanism for educating the poor; only a small group perceive citizen participation as a mechanism for generating power and influence. On the basis of this information, it would be inferred that few board members subscribe to the idea of playing an active role in determining social welfare policies.[13] However,

[12] C. Wendell King, *Social Movements in the United States* (New York: Random House, 1956), p. 70.

[13] The distinction between "active" and "passive" participation is described in Chapter II.

Clients or Constituents

Table 12

NEIGHBORHOOD BOARD MEMBERS' VIEWS ON THE
REASON FOR CITIZEN PARTICIPATION ($N = 256$)

Primary Reason for Citizen Participation	Board Members (Percentages)
To increase the influence of the poor on agencies that serve them	8.6
To facilitate communication between service agencies and the poor	44.5
To educate the poor for self-help	44.1
No information	2.8
Total	100

other information contradicts this inference: although there is no strong consensus, the evidence presented in Table 13 indicates that, regardless of their abstract view of citizen participation, a majority of the members favor an active role in decision-making.

Table 13

COMPARISON OF NEIGHBORHOOD BOARD MEMBERS' VIEWS ON THE REASONS FOR PARTICIPATION AND CITIZEN PLANNING ROLES ($N = 244$)

Reason for Citizen Participation	Preferred Role of Citizens in Planning Program		
	Active % (No.)	Passive % (No.)	Total % (No.)
To increase the influence of the poor on agencies that serve them	70 (14)	30 (6)	100 (20)
To facilitate communication between service agencies and the poor	63 (71)	37 (42)	100 (113)
To educate the poor for self-help	51 (57)	49 (54)	100 (111)

156

Internal Solidarity

These data present a picture of ideological inconsistency and confusion. The majority of the board members want to influence directly the decision-making process, but few consider citizen participation as the prime mechanism for achieving this end. Citizen participation is viewed as a mechanism to facilitate education or interaction, neither of which necessarily implies power and direct influence. However, in dealing with views and attitudes as revealed in a few questionnaire items, it is necessary to exercise caution; these "pencil and paper" attitudes have little validity or value unless they can somehow predict or explain people's behavior. The question remains, then, do the board members' actions reflect their "pencil and paper" attitudes? Are they inconsistent in deed as well as in word? An answer to this question may be found in the case study described in Chapter VI. There it was obvious that the board members wanted to directly influence certain Board of Education policies. However, when they confronted the Board of Education, participation was used more as a mechanism to facilitate communication than to exert influence—instead of negotiating, they simply debated the issues. Thus, ideological inconsistency and confusion were manifest in behavior as well as in attitude.

IMPLICATIONS

It was earlier suggested that internal solidarity is one of the key variables in a professional movement. No matter how well designed the strategies, how coherent the organizational structure, or how dedicated the professionals, unless the predisposition to cooperate exists or is created among the lay members, the basic foundation for collective action is lacking and the movement will inevitably falter.

In viewing the Pittsburgh program, three important determinants of internal solidarity were examined: congruent membership, group identification, and common ideology. Briefly, the findings were: *Congruent Membership*—From the status characteristics of neighborhood board members, it may be inferred that the social class structure of this group does not approximate that of the antipoverty movement's constituency. To the extent that differences exist in social class interests, it is plausible to assume that this leadership group is correspondingly neither forceful nor consistent in representing the interests of the poor. *Group Identification*—The consequences of this incongruent membership might be modified if board members could transcend their class interests and identify with the poor. The attitudinal characteristics of the board members, however, do not suggest a positive identification with the poor. *Common Ideology*—The attitudinal characteristics of board members indicate that although the majority of them agree on the democratization of social welfare as an objective to be realized, there is little overall agreement and much confusion on the means of achieving it. Moreover, where agreement does exist, it is generally on means that are inconsistent with the desired end.

On the basis of these findings, the conclusion is that after three years of operation the Pittsburgh program achieved, at best, a low degree of internal solidarity. This conclusion does not imply a total lack of cooperation among participants; it does suggest, however, that to attain cooperation among such members is a formidable task, that a sense of unity is lacking among them, and that the potential for internal conflict and fragmentation is high. This is broadly illustrated by the inability of the MCHR to organize a city-wide federation of antipoverty boards, and by the difficulty in getting all eight neighborhoods to negotiate collectively with agencies around particular program areas. A more specific illustration is provided by the experience of the Homewood-Brushton neighborhood board. As shown in Table 14, in three out of four categories its members possess proportionately more "high status" characteristics than the city-wide board membership average, making the Homewood-Brushton board the least congruent with the antipoverty constituency. In the fall of 1967, the legitimacy of this board was openly challenged by local "grass roots" groups, the contention being that it was predominantly an interest group for middle-class homeowners who constitute a minority segment of the community —a charge consistent with the data. The lack of internal solidarity, however, rarely manifested itself in such outbursts; its major mani-

Table 14

SELECTED STATUS CHARACTERISTICS OF NEIGHBORHOOD BOARD
MEMBERS, COMPARED TO CITY-WIDE BOARD MEMBERSHIP

	Classified as Poor	*Own Home*	*Earning Annual Income Above $5,000*	*Received Post-Secondary Education*
Hill	0	—	—	0
Northside	+	—	—	—
East Liberty-Garfield	0	—	+	0
Homewood-Brushton	0	+	+	+
Hazelwood-Glenwood	0	+	+	—
Southwest	0	—	—	—
Lawrenceville	0	0	—	0
South Oakland	—	+	+	0
City-wide board membership averages	19%	56%	57%	48%

Key

+ The neighborhood board percentage is 5 per cent or more *over* the city-wide average.

— The neighborhood board percentage is 5 per cent or more *below* the city-wide average.

0 The neighborhood board percentage is *less than* 5 per cent above or below the city-wide average.

festations were citizen inertia and subtle resistance to collective action.

Why, after almost three years of operation, was the anti-poverty movement in Pittsburgh unable to develop substantial solidarity within its constituency? Some of the answers are embedded

159

in the structure and philosophy of the city's program, whereas others relate more generally to the very nature of a professional movement. In all social reform movements, the processes of recruitment and indoctrination are essential to the development of solidarity. In a professional movement, these tasks are complicated by the fact that they are most often initiated by outsiders who can be viewed as "agents provocateurs," in contrast to indigenous rank-and-file leadership. Recruitment is a singularly arduous chore in a professional movement aimed at the poor; not only are the organizers outsiders, but the individuals they are seeking to enlist are predominantly nonparticipants. The task is difficult, but not insurmountable. Indigenous leaders may be uncovered and trained; and, through them, less articulate and less motivated members of the target population may be stimulated to participate. This process, however, is long-range, involving a concentrated commitment of time and energy, with no guaranteed payoff.

The MCHR, though committed in principle to the idea of maximum feasible participation, in practice made only a superficial effort to realize this objective. From the very outset, the bulk of Pittsburgh's antipoverty resources went into the development of program services, whereas community organization, along with other functions, was placed in the hands of the generally understaffed neighborhood coordination units. The organizers thus had neither the time nor the resources to launch an intensive recruitment drive—which vitiated against the development of solidarity. Another, perhaps more crucial, factor compounded the difficulties. As stated by one neighborhood board in an evaluation of the community organization effort: "One problem of developing citizen participation is that often a hard-working citizen is hired by an OEO agency in a nonprofessional status and then can no longer serve on the board. Thus the turnover on the board is great and many of the leading citizens can no longer contribute to the board's functioning."[14] In the community-action vernacular, this process is commonly referred to as "creaming." Most of the nonprofessional

[14] Citizen's Board of Southwest Pittsburgh, *Program Evaluation of Neighborhood Coordination,* June 1967, p. 1 (mimeographed).

positions in the Pittsburgh program required that the candidate be both poor and a resident of a target neighborhood; hence, through these jobs, the most responsible, articulate, and enterprising individuals were skimmed off the pool of talent available in the low-income groups. They were usually the same indigenous leaders who might have provided an organizing link to the neighborhood—except that they were not hired as organizers! More than 90 per cent of Pittsburgh's nonprofessionals worked for service agencies; they were incorporated into the bottom rungs of the very system that the neighborhood boards wanted to influence—and the nonprofessionals were rarely in positions of influence. Once employed by service agencies, their participation on neighborhood boards entailed distinct conflicts of interest. Few agency supervisors looked with favor upon the prospect of being evaluated by their nonprofessional assistants, and few boards could depend upon the objectivity of their newly mobile members.[15]

The process of "creaming" is endemic to the antipoverty movement. However, this process is not inherently detrimental to the development of solidarity. The consequences could be the very opposite. As organizers, nonprofessionals are often better equipped than the professionals for recruiting low-income participants, securing their trust, and activating their will to cooperate.[16] The crucial factor is not the hiring of indigenous leaders, but the capacity in which they are employed. In Pittsburgh, the philosophy and structure of the program dictated that these individuals be skimmed off to expedite services rather than to organize a movement. As a result, whatever time and effort went into recruitment and indoctrination were quickly dissipated.

[15] During the Spring of 1967, the time at which data on board members were collected, 242 resident nonprofessionals were employed in the Pittsburgh program, a majority of whom had previously been board members.

[16] The implications of nonprofessionals as both organizers and expediters are discussed by Frank Riessman, "Anti-Poverty Programs and the Role of the Poor," *Poverty in America,* ed. Margaret S. Gordon (San Francisco: Chandler, 1965), pp. 403–412. Also see Mobilization For Youth, Inc., *Action on the Lower East Side* (New York: Mobilization For Youth, 1964), pp. 147–155; and Perry Levinson and Jeffry Schiller, "Role Analysis of the Indigenous Nonprofessional," *Social Work,* 1966, 2(3), pp. 95–101.

CHAPTER IX

Goal Achievement

The democratization of social welfare is one of the more radical reform objectives of the antipoverty movement. There is little evidence that the Pittsburgh program was at all successful in achieving this objective. The reasons for this result emerge clearly in an examination of five key elements of goal achievement in a professional movement—structure, strategy, professional leadership, solidarity, and opposition. In the preceding chapters each of these elements was analyzed relative to the Pittsburgh program. A brief review of the general conclusions follows.

162

Goal Achievement

Structure. In the early stages of development, care was taken to allocate resources in a manner that did not rupture the "status quo"; few jurisdictions were invaded except that of the citizens, who played almost no part in the planning phase. In attempting to satisfy local welfare agency interests, the program was built more as a conduit for the expeditious delivery of services than as a platform from which to launch a citizens' movement for deep-seated social reform. The democratization of social welfare was not relinquished as an objective, but it was pushed into the background. In addition, the Community Action Agency was structured in a manner that more strongly identified it with the interests of the Negro community than with those of the generic poor, and this structure had negative implications for the eventual development of broad-based solidarity among all the potential constituents.

Strategy. Citizen participation was built into the structure as a mechanism for social change. It was infused with courageous rhetoric about "citizen planning" and "citizen evaluation"; but, as actually implemented, it offered the opportunity for little more than a rubber-stamp ratification of plans and programs by citizens. Later, attempts were made to alter this mode of participation. These efforts faltered, partly because structural constraints and the lack of solidarity inhibited collective action. Also, the MCHR was quite hesitant to assume a forceful role as an advocate of the poor.

Professional Leadership. From the outset, the professional organizers were in a tenuous position, one which did not provide the latitude for organizing a vocal constituency. They were tied to a structure that required a division of loyalty—to citizens, to delegate agencies, and to the MCHR. Furthermore, their role as coordinator-organizers contained inherent conflicts, which vitiated against a really forcible approach to citizen participation; it called for dealing with both service agencies and citizens on an equal basis.

Solidarity. The inability to achieve collective action was not caused solely by the limitations of the professionals. The lay leadership itself was not predisposed to cooperate in such ventures. They did not perceive themselves as representing a coherent group whose interests were at stake; their characteristics were not those of an in-

163

terest group representing the poor; and they did not agree upon the meaning of citizen participation as a strategy for social change. Here, too, the consequences of a service-oriented structure were felt. Non-professionals were almost always employed in positions of service dispensation rather than of citizen organization. This frustrated recruitment efforts; as soon as low-income leaders were found and nurtured, they were hired by agencies and effectively disengaged from citizen participation.

Opposition. Each of the above elements contributed to the development of a program that was relatively nonthreatening to both the established welfare institutions and the community leaders; the general public was lulled by the favorable press image, and the employment incentive and identification with a "successful" program inhibited citizen criticism. Thus, the emphasis upon an ameliorative objective—providing services to the poor—rather than structural reform evoked virtually no organized opposition, and the program was able to flourish in a benign environment.

Together, these five elements depict the dynamics of goal displacement. The democratization of social welfare was not rejected as a legitimate goal; it was simply not vigorously pursued. The Pittsburgh program concentrated on achieving a more moderate objective, and it was quite successful at realizing this goal. The program did provide a beginning for many needed services to the poor; Legal Aid, Upward Bound, Head Start, and Day Care were a few of the more excellent services offered through the antipoverty system. However, the poor remained as clients with little influence over the institutions that served them.

Within the general context of social movement, the process of goal displacement is often considered a prerequisite to organizational survival. Peter Blau suggests:

> The major interest of party or union officials is to strengthen the organization, not only because their jobs depend upon its survival, but also because a powerful machine is needed in the fight for the intended reform. In this respect the self-interest of the leadership and the collective interests of the membership coincide. Officials, consequently, are willing to make great sacrifices

for the sake of fortifying the organization. To attract more members, they will abandon unpopular points of the program. To prevent the possibility of a crushing defeat, they will fail to enforce union demands by calling a strike. "Thus, from a means, organization becomes an end." Step by step, the original objectives are surrendered in the interest of increased organizational strength.[1]

Relating this idea to the antipoverty movement, Melvin Mogulof, a Regional Manager of Community Action Programs for the Office of Economic Opportunity, writes:

> Those who are enraptured with "innovation" and "social change" must also recognize that it is crucial for the community-action agency to deal initially with the need to establish and maintain itself. It must demonstrate its credibility as an agency by winning funds; it must legitimate itself with the organizations in its environment (some of whom have won their own legitimacy by creating the illusion of effectively dealing with the problems of poverty).[2]

Both men state, however, that this initial tendency towards goal displacement is not insurmountable. Blau notes the possibility of a "succession of goals; as earlier objectives are attained, they become stepping stones for new ones."[3] Mogulof applies this hypothesis to the antipoverty movement: "During the first organizational phase of a CAP it is entirely normal for the concepts of 'establishment' and 'maintenance' to dominate the agency's efforts . . . . this first phase can and will lead to a second phase in which the language—characterized by words such as 'social change' and 'innovation'—will furnish appropriate (even mandatory) concepts to apply to the community-action idea." He notes that a principal characteristic of citizen participation in Phase I is that delegates are chosen by the nonpoor to represent the poor; but Phase II "should see movement

[1] Peter Blau, *Bureaucracy in Modern Society* (New York: Random House, 1956), p. 93.
[2] Melvin B. Mogulof, "A Developmental Approach to the Community Action Idea," *Social Work,* 1967, *12*(2), p. 14.
[3] Blau, p. 95.

towards a process of potential beneficiary groups selecting their own representatives" and "the establishment of area councils composed of poor people who will be given the authority to veto program inputs for their neighborhoods."[4]

Over a period of two and one-half years, from the winter of 1964 to the summer of 1967, the Pittsburgh program established its credibility and legitimacy through the development of a multi-million-dollar service system. In this respect, the service objective was substantially realized. However, by July 1965, funds were becoming scarce; and it began to be obvious that, barring a change in Congressional policy, further service expansion was limited.

DISPLACEMENT OR SUCCESSION?

It is difficult to ascertain the future direction of the Pittsburgh program. It has established credibility and achieved a legitimate position in the city's welfare system. Will it become more firmly institutionalized and take a place alongside the traditional dispensers of welfare services? Or will it assume a more radical posture and advocate the democratization and reform of social welfare? The answers to these questions are not clear. Obviously, external forces, over which the leaders in Pittsburgh have relatively little control—for example, the elimination by Congress of the antipoverty program—may determine the final course of events. However, excluding such drastic events, the direction taken in Pittsburgh will be predominantly determined by the MCHR.

A few clues to this direction are provided by certain events that occurred toward the middle of 1967. In September, the Executive Director of the MCHR issued a memorandum to the staff, outlining goals and directions for 1968; he stated that the major thrusts of the program were to be in the three areas of employment services, planning and evaluation, and citizen participation. Concerning citizen participation, the Executive Director noted:

> In the past we have been working with advisory committees and citizen councils who have helped in giving direction to the pro-

[4] Mogulof, pp. 14–15.

gram and formulating policy. However, for the most part, it has been a small identifiable few who have been the sustaining power and influence in the entire community-action movement. It is hoped that this base will be more effective, that it will move from the rung of the articulate middle class and working class with strong middle-class values who have to a great extent given leadership to the program, down to the roots of those who have little, who have low-income . . . In order to do this, it will be necessary to have more staff at the Mayor's Committee on Human Resources, Inc. and more staff in the neighborhoods with specific responsibilities of involving low-income people in the daily process of community action.[5]

In line with this objective, the central staff budget for 1968 included positions for forty nonprofessionals to work as organizers in the target neighborhoods, which represented almost a threefold increase in organizing staff. This increase occurred at a time when all service programs, except employment, were being held constant or cut back. Another proposed objective was the expansion of employment services, to be achieved via an MCHR-controlled Concentrated Employment Program. These plans marked the beginning of two important changes in the Pittsburgh program: a shift in the allocation of resources toward community organization (see Figure 2), and a move away from the delegate agency structure toward a direct delivery of services by the MCHR.

A few weeks after the above memorandum was circulated, an all-day conference was held to explore further the program's future. At this meeting there was a general consensus that the delegate-agency structure for coordination should be eliminated and coordination staff placed directly under the MCHR's administration. The difficulties in accomplishing this reorganization were clearly recognized—specifically, the resistance that could be expected from most delegate agencies and from some citizens' groups. However, it was also understood that if the proposed positions for forty nonprofessional organizers were contracted out to the delegate agencies, their vested interests and their power would increase pro-

[5] Memorandum from the Executive Director of the Mayor's Committee on Human Resources, September 8, 1967, p. 3.

FIGURE 2. ALLOCATION OF OEO GRANTS BY PROGRAM
AREAS, 1965–1967

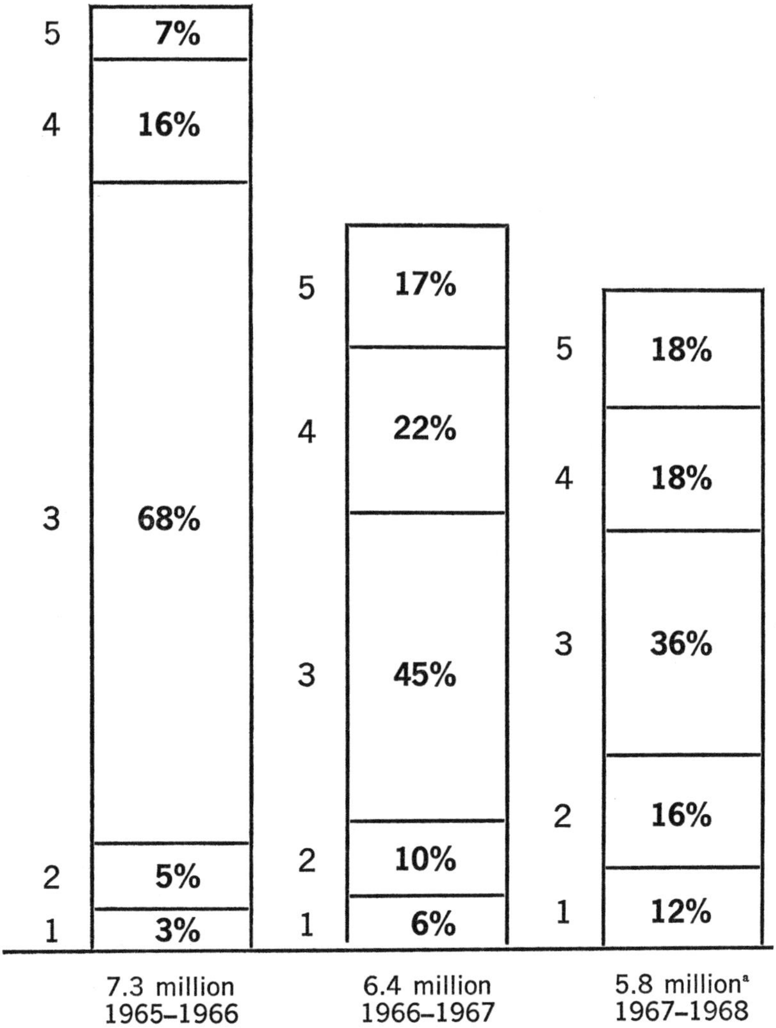

5	7%		
4	16%		
3	68%		
2	5%		
1	3%		

5	17%
4	22%
3	45%
2	10%
1	6%

5	18%
4	18%
3	36%
2	16%
1	12%

7.3 million   6.4 million   5.8 million[a]
1965–1966   1966–1967   1967–1968

[a] Estimate based upon 2.9 million allocation for 6 months.

KEY
1. Central Administration
2. Coordination—Community Organization
3. Education
4. Welfare and Social Services
5. Health, Legal, Employment, and Housing

portionately, and reorganization would be even more difficult to achieve thereafter.

Shortly afterward, a meeting was held with the neighborhood coordinators, during which the MCHR staff cautiously broached the subject of centralizing coordination. The coordinators were almost unanimous in support of the general idea, seeing the social-action potential of a consolidation of their efforts; but when it came to specifics, they were not unanimous or clear about the organizational auspices of the consolidation, and their uncertainty focused especially on the MCHR. Nevertheless, the idea was gaining momentum, if only in the abstract.

Another incident that occurred at this time is worth recounting. Although minor, it indicates a change in the MCHR's relationship with the more radical citizens' organizations. The MCHR staff had supported sub rosa the efforts of city-wide organizations that had grown out of the neighborhood councils, such as Citizens Against Slum Housing (CASH) and Citizens Against Inadequate Resources (CAIR). Early in October 1967, CAIR was planning public hearings to protest against proposed federal welfare legislation. In response to these plans, the Executive Director of the MCHR sent a memorandum to the neighborhood coordinators and presidents of citizens' councils, granting permission to use activity funds for transportation and stating that the agency "strongly backs this endeavor."[6] Unlike prior times, the MCHR this time allowed its sentiment and its commitment to surface; its staff openly identified themselves with the social-action reform groups.

The evidence is, to be sure, incomplete; it provides, at best, a clue that the Pittsburgh program may be seriously starting to press for the democratization of social welfare. But organizing the poor to influence the institutions that serve them is no simple task. There are many obstacles to overcome before this goal is achieved, and some of them—such as apathy and parochialism—are embedded in the participants themselves. The question, then, of

[6] Memorandum from the Executive Director of the Mayor's Committee on Human Resources, Inc., October 4, 1967.

169

whether or not the initial displacement of radical reformist objectives will result in a succession of goals will be answered in the near future. Given the will, the democratization and reform of social welfare can develop only if the way is very carefully charted. If the program embarks upon this course, it must contend with two immediate and fundamental issues—the professional role in social reform and the legitimacy of neighborhood representation. These issues have implications for the immediate future of Pittsburgh's antipoverty movement and possibly the future of similar professional reform movements in other cities.

PROFESSIONAL REFORM

In Pittsburgh the professionals on central staff and in the field were the main actors in constructing an organizational framework, proposing strategies, providing leadership, and manipulating the conditions that gave rise to whatever degrees of solidarity and opposition emerged. During the program's first three years, citizens' groups made some proposals and demands; but even in these actions the strong mark of professional instigation was distinguishable. The "voice of the people" was often an act of ventriloquism, and it was a voice rarely heard on basic decisions made during this period. The consequences of professional leadership and control produced few vibrations because the issues raised were not volcanic. The program was operating from a service orientation. Thus, questions arose concerning staff requirements, logistical strategy for service delivery, theoretical numbers to be served, social service agency jurisdictions, and the like. These issues did not preclude bureaucratic in-fighting, but overall the challenge to established social welfare institutions was mild. As long as no bone-shattering issues emerged to alter the established structure, the antipoverty professionals could act with impunity.

However, what will happen when the issues become more controversial? Can the professional sustain his position of leadership while initiating, for example, an effort to force public school decentralization, or some other measure of equal potential for controversy? The antipoverty professionals are not independent agents.

170

Goal Achievement

They are sponsored, that is paid and sanctioned, by the MCHR Board of Directors and must operate within the policy guidelines established by this body. The MCHR Board is composed of individuals representing diverse interests. Most of the board members representing political and social welfare institutions vigorously support the agency's service orientation; they are not to be counted among the champions of social action and institutional change. These institutional representatives have the power to exercise considerable influence over agency policy. They not only outnumber those members who would support professional advocacy for welfare reforms, but they also outweigh them on the scales of economic and political influence.[7] This influence was rarely exerted during the program's first three years because the major issues dealt with programmatic variables that were almost devoid of political implications. It is improbable that these institutional representatives would act with the same equanimity if the antipoverty professionals began openly advocating measures for deep-seated reform. Thus the existing organizational structure contains inherent restraints upon professional involvement with citizens' action groups. As long as the professional's sponsorship resides in the Community Action Agency, his role is likely to be circumscribed in the implementation of reformist objectives. Professionals might surreptitiously advise indigenous action groups, but the citizen participants would have to assume a larger share of initiative and leadership for such groups to flourish. Judging from the few experiences in Pittsburgh, the prognosis for this eventuality is not encouraging. When professional support was withdrawn, citizens' groups began to atrophy.

Any efforts to implement reformist objectives must also

[7] Under the Economic Opportunity Act Amendments of 1967, state, county, and city governments were offered the option of either incorporating Community Action Agencies within their governmental structures or of designating other groups to fill this role. Although very few local governments chose to change existing Community Action Agency auspices, these amendments served to symbolize and reaffirm their authority. Also included in these amendments was the requirement that Community Action Agency boards consist of one-third poor people with the remaining membership divided equally between public officials and representatives from the private sector.

171

contend with the issue of neighborhood representation. Who speaks for the poor? This question was given scant consideration in the first few years of Pittsburgh's antipoverty movement. The neighborhood council officially recognized by the MCHR was accepted as the voice of that community in antipoverty affairs. As the data on the composition of these council boards indicate, the members were not characteristically representative of low-income neighborhood residents. Also, they were selected through processes that would not make them of necessity accountable to their neighbors.[8] In its final translation, citizen participation meant the participation of an elite group of activists under the general leadership of professional organizers. This arrangement bears little resemblance to the participatory democracy that antipoverty workers were supposed to stimulate among low-income neighborhood residents.

The legitimacy of neighborhood councils claiming to represent anything more than self-sanctioning groups of citizen activists was open to serious debate. This question was sometimes alluded to by institutional representatives and often privately discussed among antipoverty professionals. But in three years it became a concrete public issue on only one occasion, and then with regard to only one neighborhood, the reason being that a somewhat fragile, but nevertheless functional, modus operandi had been established between the MCHR, professional organizers, institutional representatives, and neighborhood council members. To have opened a debate over the legitimacy of neighborhood representation would have precipitated a major crisis in service program operations. The yearly funding process, which itself bordered on a crisis condition, would have been totally disrupted while citizens' councils were being reorganized. And any attempted reorganization of neighborhood councils promised to open its own Pandora's box of intra-neighborhood strife. Thus, as long as the focus of citizen participa-

---

[8] With regard to the legitimacy of neighborhood representation, a comparative study of five Community Action Programs in California indicates that low accountability and high rates of participation by nonpoor residents are not at all unique to Pittsburgh. See Ralph Kramer, *Participation of the Poor* (Englewood Cliffs, N.J.: Prentice-Hall, 1969), pp. 188–200,

tion was on the minutiae of programmatic detailing, the legitimacy of neighborhood spokesmen was a moot issue. However, it is highly doubtful that institutional representatives would continue to respond to this veneer of democracy as an authentic product if the neighborhood spokesmen started demanding structural reforms in the name of the community. Indeed, at this point, the issue of who speaks for the poor, how the spokesmen were selected, and to whom they are accountable is likely to receive considerable scrutiny.

Of these two impending issues, the role of the professional presents the most formidable challenge. In order to advocate social reform and openly exercise leadership in this cause, professional sponsorship must be disengaged from local political and social welfare institutions. This requirement cannot be met within the existing organizational context of the antipoverty movement. Although the professional is a necessary ingredient in a movement for social welfare reform through citizen participation, such a movement must also stir the constituents whom it ostensibly represents. The issue here is not entirely one of numbers. Active participants in any reform movement usually consist of only a small fraction of the groups represented. The vast majority of people in these groups are supportive members to whom the activists are accountable. Supportive members have a conscious stake in the movement's objectives and occasionally can be called upon to stand up and be counted. The activists work closely with the professionals in sustaining an organization on a day-to-day basis. The antipoverty movement was effective in recruiting and began to train an activist minority, but failed to develop a base of supportive membership in the neighborhoods. Unless this base of concern for social change (whether its locus be geographic or around functional problem areas) is broadened and those who claim to speak for the poor are also formally accountable to the poor, the prospects are faint that citizen participation, regardless of its organizational sponsorship, will provide the sufficient impulse for the democratization and reform of social welfare.

$\mathcal{A}$PPENDIX

Notes on Method

$\mathbb{H}$ow does one study a professional movement? At its origin and through its early developmental stages, such a movement exists primarily in the mind of the viewer. Most of the professional and lay participants in Pittsburgh's antipoverty program did not perceive themselves as part of a nation-wide, or even a city-wide, reform movement; their visions extended little beyond the narrow neighborhood and programmatic aspects with which they were immediately involved. Few saw the broad structural and functional relationships between the numerous groups across the city or the interrelationships between the elements of which the program was composed. One reason why I undertook this study was my perception, after working with various aspects of the program, of this lack of understanding. If this understanding could be provided through my study, there might be a more rational basis for both citizen and professional decision-making in the future.

The study covers the first three and one-half years of Pittsburgh's antipoverty program, from the planning stages in mid-1964 to the early part of 1968. During the period when I conducted the actual research, from the fall of 1966 through the winter of 1967, I was employed as a staff member in the Research Division of the Mayor's Committee on Human Resources, Inc., Pittsburgh's official Community Action Agency. Prior to this period, I had done two years of field work as a community organization student at the University of Pittsburgh Graduate School of Social Work and was, for a short time, employed by ACTION-Housing, Inc. Through these various positions I had, at one time or another, worked with citizens' groups in Homewood-Brushton, East Liberty-Garfield, Lawrenceville, and the North Side, four of the eight antipoverty neighborhoods, and had contact with most of the relevant welfare-related institutions and individuals. Moreover, my wife was employed as the assistant coordinator for the North Side antipoverty program from 1965 to 1967. Thus, when I embarked upon the study, I was in a particularly strategic position to enter the system as a participant-observer: I had already established a number of friendly relationships with citizens from antipoverty neighborhoods; I had made numerous social as well as professional contacts with the program's staff; and finally, my position at the MCHR allowed me to observe certain events, such as professional staff meetings and executive sessions of the MCHR Board, to which an outsider might have had difficulty gaining access.

In this study, I relied most heavily on data derived from participant observation; in addition, data were collected from program-related documents, and from a survey of 256 citizen board members and 26 professional staff conducted in the spring of 1967. Numerous informal interviews were also held with key staff and citizens. This multiple approach was taken in part because of the supposition that:

> Once a proposition has been confirmed by two or more independent measurement processes, the uncertainty of its interpretation is greatly reduced. The most persuasive evidence comes through a triangulation of measurement processes. If a proposition can survive the onslaught of a series of imperfect measures, with all their irrelevant error, confidence should be placed in it.[1]

Also, no one of these techniques could provide all of the data that I considered necessary for a vivid analysis of the antipoverty movement in Pittsburgh. The following is a brief discussion of these techniques and how they were employed throughout the study.

PARTICIPANT OBSERVATION

When sociology as an academic discipline was still being nourished in the womb of philosophy, participant observation was advocated by Saint Simon as a method for gaining a precise understanding of the various classes of society.[2] As a research technique it affords the investigator an opportunity to go beyond statistical and historical description, to probe beneath the surface of the system of interaction under analysis, and to become involved and to some extent identified with the people and events he is studying. Identification has certain negative ramifications in terms of objectivity, as illustrated by William Whyte's experience while study-

[1] Eugene Webb, Donald T. Campbell, Richard D. Schwartz, and Lee Sechrest, *Unobtrusive Measures: Nonreactive Research in the Social Sciences* (Chicago: Rand McNally, 1966), p. 3. The authors provide an imaginative and highly entertaining exposition of this viewpoint and some interesting comments on observational techniques.

[2] Frank E. Manuel, *The New World of Henri St. Simon* (Notre Dame, Ind.: University of Notre Dame Press, 1963), pp. 90–94. (There is some evidence to indicate that Saint Simon often behaved in a less than saintly manner, and that he advocated the idea of participant observation mainly to justify his eccentric habits in terms of scientific endeavors.)

ing the social life of "corner boys" in Boston's North End. At one point in the course of this investigation, he moved from the role of participant observer to that of an active participant, organizing a citizens' march on city hall to protest the lack of hot water in the local bathhouse.[3] Similarly, Kurt and Gladys Lang report how two members of their research team "made their decision for Christ" while observing a Billy Graham crusade.[4]

Although research findings are sometimes perceived as if the investigation were conducted in a state of pure clinical detachment, social scientists, like other human beings, carry with them sets of preconceived notions that guide their perceptions of reality. When data are collected through the use of objective instruments, this bias may emerge in the analysis. In participant observation, however, the researcher is both the instrument and the analyst. Thus the problem is twofold, in that the researcher may tend to systematically block out as well as misinterpret the events he is studying. There is no way to eliminate this bias totally, but it may be minimized if, at the outset, the investigator identifies the personal values and attitudes that might influence his research effort. In this regard I should state, briefly, that in general my sentiments favor expanding welfare services and creating a more equitable distribution of power, opportunities, and benefits in American society. I do not believe that good intentions alone can achieve this sort of redistribution; the economic resources of this country are such that poverty could be virtually willed out of existence, yet it persists. I think that something more than good will is needed, specifically, political power; and that one way to gain this power is through organizing deprived groups for collective action. This view asserts that in a democratic pluralistic society, the poor, as members of legitimate interest groups, have a right to exercise proportionate influence in

[3] Whyte admits that he tried to rationalize this effort by attempting to convince himself that he was conducting an experiment. See William Whyte, *Street Corner Society* (Chicago: University of Chicago Press, 1943), pp. 337–341.

[4] Kurt Lang and Gladys Lang, "Decisions for Christ: Billy Graham in New York City," *Identity and Anxiety*, ed. Maurice Stein, Arthur J. Vidich, and David M. White (Glencoe, Ill.: Free Press, 1960), p. 425.

decision-making processes, particularly with respect to the institutions that serve them; the view further urges that this right be facilitated.

While conducting this study, I attempted to minimize the imposition of my personal views in the collection and analysis of observational data in three ways: (1) reflecting upon alternative explanations of the events and actions that took place, (2) trying to perceive these events and actions from the perspectives of the various individuals involved, and (3) seeking to observe situations that might offer some degree of comparability.[5] I cannot, however, claim that these precautions were systematically applied or that my value judgments did not enter into the interpretations that emerged. Heeding Herbert Gans' suggestion, I endeavored to be "as objective as humanly possible, not by renouncing value judgments, but by refraining from hasty and oversimplified ones, and by showing why people behave as they do, especially when this behavior violates prevalent norms."[6]

In addition to the problem of the researcher as a biased instrument, there is the problem of the effects of this instrument upon the subject to which it is applied.[7] Simply stated, the dilemma is that the very presence of the investigator may introduce changes in the action being studied, for which there are no systematic controls. In participant observation these effects are almost unavoidable; but again, the researcher may take conscious precautions to minimize

[5] As an example of comparability, many of the observations discussed in Chapter VI were matched against another case of confederated effort, in the evaluation of the Allegheny County Health Department program. I chose to use the Board of Education case because the planning with citizens was more involved, the issues were more clearly defined, the results more definite, and the interaction more lively. However, in terms of citizen participation, I might easily have substituted the Health Department experience without altering the substance of the process described.

[6] Herbert J. Gans, *The Urban Villagers* (New York: Free Press, 1962). p. 346. In this section of the book, Gans provides a brief but pointed analysis of the types and problems of participant observation.

[7] This problem is sometimes described as the "control effect." It is classically illustrated in the Hawthorne studies. See Matilda W. Riley, *Sociological Research: I. A Case Study Approach* (New York: Harcourt, 1963), pp. 71, 626–629.

them. For example, in the case study described in Chapter VI, I was interested in contacting a group of citizens to find out if and how they had followed up on the recommendations they had made to the Board of Education, or if they were aware of any action that had been taken in accordance with these recommendations. This was three months after the citizens had met with the Board of Education, and I knew that the actions taken so far were not acceptable; that is, a job description had been developed, but it did not incorporate the citizens' recommendations. In asking the citizens these questions, would I remind them of an incident that they had perhaps already forgotten, or even stimulate them to take further steps that might alter the otherwise natural course of events? This problem was complicated by the fact that my personal sentiments in this situation favored increasing the citizens' pressure upon the Board of Education. There was no way to resolve the dilemma. But in an attempt to minimize the effects of interjecting a "foreign" element into the system, I considered how the questions might be phrased to keep them innocuously inquisitive rather than challenging; for example, "I was wondering whether you had heard about . . . ." rather than "Did you make any attempts to find out. . . ." Also, I made an effort to keep the interviews short and not to reveal my motives.

However, in terms of my role as a participant observer, this example is more the exception than the rule. As a member of the MCHR staff, my behavior was principally that of a "real" participant. Although I did not shed the role of an observer, my actions throughout the study period were dictated, essentially, by the rights and responsibilities afforded the status of a central staff person. At meetings with both citizens and staff, I was obliged to voice my views and to present suggestions. And thus it was often difficult to minimize whatever impact my presence might have had in certain situations.

These are some of the limitations in the collection and analysis of the observational data that I used throughout the study, and principally in developing Chapters IV, V, and VI. As a final note in relation to this method, I might suggest that, if the pitfalls inherent in the use of participant observation are many, the rewards are at least consonant with the risks; for it is the only technique that affords the investigator an opportunity to get a glimpse of reality through the eyes of those he is studying.

Between March and May of 1967, I conducted two surveys as a special MCHR project on citizen participation. One focused upon the citizen board members of the eight neighborhood councils and the other upon agency staff, chosen on the basis of their operational proximity to the citizens' groups and their administrative responsibility for programs. For each service program I attempted to select the highest administrative staff members dealing on a face-to-face basis with the citizen committees. These surveys were made for two major reasons. First, I wanted some quantitative data against which to test certain observations. In addition, there were a number of important questions concerning attitudes and demographic characteristics for which the observational data alone did not provide sufficient answers and which, anyway, were needed by the MCHR.

Thirty-two individuals were selected for the staff survey, based upon my judgments concerning the administrative functions of program personnel and the regularity with which they interacted with citizens. The questionnaires were mailed out to this group, and the return was approximately 82 per cent (26). The citizens' survey was more complex. Here I was interested in tapping not the occasional or one-shot participant who might have come to a single meeting and had his name recorded on a membership roster, but the population of active participants who were in a position actually to influence decision-making on the neighborhood level. Thus, this survey was focused primarily upon the members of the neighborhood boards. Six of the eight neighborhoods had "elected" boards ranging in membership from thirty to sixty individuals, all of whom were included in the survey. The other two neighborhoods had "open" boards, in which every person coming to any meeting was counted as a member, so that at any given time their membership lists might number from 200 to 400 individuals. Rather than attempting to survey all of these people, many of whom were occasional or one-shot participants, I elected to survey populations in these neighborhoods consisting of the members of the executive committees and ten of the otherwise most active board members. In determining who the most active board members were, I relied upon the judgments of the coordination staff in these neighborhoods.

After these decisions were made, one of the major difficulties was to pinpoint the constantly shifting population. Many of the membership lists were outdated by the time I received them; some participants had died, others had moved away, and a few had resigned. In the three months during which the survey was conducted, one council held an election, adding new members. Thus, throughout the process, these lists were in a constant state of revision. In the final count there were 297 individuals in the survey population.

As the citizen questionnaires were anonymous, I did not want to conduct this survey by mail because, if the returns were low, it would have been extremely difficult to do a follow-up. Thus, the initial plan was to use members of the Volunteers in Service to America (VISTA) corps working in the eight neighborhoods to administer the survey. These individuals would deliver the questionnaires to the citizens' homes and then return a few days later to pick them up. Prior to this, the citizens would receive a letter from the MCHR explaining the purpose of the survey and asking for their cooperation. This way I would be able to keep track of those who did not respond and follow up on them with a second effort. As the survey covered a very broad geographic area and the VISTA workers were not uniformly reliable, there were some difficulties. The initial returns were lower than I had anticipated, and I spent more than a month on the follow-up, recontacting citizens and administering questionnaires, in the field. After the follow-up, a final effort was made through the mail, which assured anonymity to those who might not have responded because of concern about being identified as the questionnaires were collected. In the end, 256 questionnaires had been collected, representing approximately 86 per cent of the total survey population. I was confident of having reached the population of active participants because of the questionnaire response on the subject of meeting attendance: 49 per cent claimed to have attended at least four meetings a month during the previous six months, 38 per cent claimed one to three meetings a month for this period, and only 12 per cent claimed an attendance rate of less than one meeting a month.

The fact that the survey was conducted out of the MCHR imbued this effort with "political" overtones, which are important when considering the possibility of biased responses. Certainly the respondents showed some concern about how this information would be used. One citizen flatly refused to participate because he thought the information would be employed to discredit the neighborhood councils; a few were less direct in their refusal to participate, but evaded all follow-up efforts in a manner that suggested something more than coincidence.

In general, however, most of the respondents were quite cooperative as evidenced by the fact that only 4.7 per cent refused to give their income, always a difficult piece of information to obtain. It appeared that they viewed the survey primarily as an opportunity to register their real thoughts and opinions, which, as illustrated by the following remark, were sometimes not especially flattering: "I am a simple soul and I am always being asked to fill something out for you people down there. Why don't you call yourselves the Mayor's Computers? Because that's all you are doing."

The survey data were used primarily in Chapter VIII to analyze membership characteristics relevant to solidarity. They were also used in parts of Chapters IV, V, and VII to describe citizen and staff attitudes.

PROGRAM-RELATED DOCUMENTS

I systematically reviewed four main sources of written information: citizen evaluations, memoranda, minutes, and newspaper articles: (a) *Citizen evaluations*—All of the written evaluations submitted by citizens' councils to the MCHR over a three-year period were analyzed with a number of questions in mind. What types of program changes did the citizens ask for? How much consensus did the evaluations reflect concerning problem areas? Did the same problems emerge year after year? (b) *Memoranda*—Starting from the very beginning of the program, all of the in-house and inter-agency memoranda, particularly those from the Office of Economic Opportunity, were examined, with a view toward ascertaining any shifts in policy towards citizen participation. (c) *Minutes*—The minutes of all the MCHR Board of Directors meetings and central staff meetings were reviewed for content. These documents were also used to determine attendance at meetings, particularly that of the citizen board members. (d) *Newspaper articles*—The Public Information Division of the MCHR keeps a file of all the articles concerning the War on Poverty that appear in the local press. This file was used for the purpose of determining the coverage that Pittsburgh's antipoverty program received from the city's two major newspapers. A content analysis was made of 140 articles appearing in these newspapers between March 1966 and May 1967. The criteria used for this analysis and its results are reported in Chapter VII.

In addition to these sources, my position at the MCHR afforded access to letters, reports, and other documents. The information contained therein was usually followed up and cross-checked through informal interviews. The data for most of Chapter III and parts of Chapters IV, V, and VII were drawn from program-related documents.

Index

A

ACTION-Housing, Inc., 59; and co-ordination contracts, 57–58, 64, 106; development of, 45; and Neighborhood Urban Extension, 45–46, 46n, 57–58, 106, 139; staff of, 43, 46, 62, 71, 72, 176

ALINSKY, S., 5, 5n

Architects of Pittsburgh CAP, 13n, 43–44, 46, 48, 138–140

ASCH, S. E., 114n

B

BARNARD, C., 82, 82n

BARR, J. M. *See* Mayor's office

BELLAS, D., 103n

BELLUSH, J., 81n

BERELSON, B., 149n

BLAU, P., 39n, 77n, 164–165, 165n

Board of Directors, MCHR, 91, 171; and city-wide leadership vacuum, 102–105, 133; functions of regarding funds and programs, 109, 124; letters to, 95n, 109n, 125n, 184; meetings of, 103, 132, 176, 184; members of, 53, 58–61, 67–68, 102n, 133, 134, 138, 143, 171; minutes of, 60n, 61n, 184; Personnel Selection Committee of, 61–63; presentation to by Hazelwood citizens, 103n; type of representation on, 143

Board of Public Education (Pittsburgh), 48, 52, 59, 85, 126–127; and confederated citizens (case study), 110–128; Elementary and Secondary Education Act, 111, 113, 125; Head Start, 82, 111, 164; Kindergarten Aides, 110–128 passim; members of, 118–119; and Negro community, 47–48; Oliver High School, 114; school-community agents, 95–97, 110–128 passim; staff team of, 112–115, 114n, 117–118, 120; superintendent of, 113, 114n, 124, 125, 125n

BOONE, R., 14

Brashear Association, 58

BREDEMEIR, H. C., 4n

BROWN, B., 59, 61

BRYMER, R. A., 5n

Buhl Foundation, 45

C

CAHN, E. S., 26n, 27, 33, 33n

CAHN, J. C., 26n, 33, 33n

CAMERON, W. B., 15n, 153, 153n

CAMPBELL, D. T., 177n

CARTWRIGHT, D., 34n

Catholic Diocese of Pittsburgh, 48, 59, 85, 103, 134

CENTERS, R., 154, 154n

CICCO, J., 48

Citizen participation: in community action, 31–33, 111, 136, 146, 170, 172; criteria of, 31; forms of (active-passive continuum), 12, 13, 31–33; in Pittsburgh,